Ethical Approaches to Preaching

Ethical Approaches to Preaching

Choosing the Best Way to Preach
About Difficult Issues

John S. McClure

 CASCADE *Books* • Eugene, Oregon

ETHICAL APPROACHES TO PREACHING
Choosing the Best Way to Preach About Difficult Issues

Cascade Books
An Imprint of Wipf and Stock Publishers
199 W. 8th Ave., Suite 3
Eugene, OR 97401

www.wipfandstock.com

PAPERBACK ISBN: 978-1-7252-7453-2
HARDCOVER ISBN: 978-1-7252-7454-9
EBOOK ISBN: 978-1-7252-7455-6

Cataloguing-in-Publication data:

Names: McClure, John S., author.

Title: Ethical approaches to preaching : choosing the best way to preach
about difficult issues / by John S. McClure.

Description: Eugene, OR: Cascade Books, 2021 | Includes bibliographi-
cal references.

Identifiers: ISBN 978-1-7252-7453-2 (paperback) | ISBN 978-1-7252-
7454-9 (hardcover) | ISBN 978-1-7252-7455-6 (ebook)

Subjects: LCSH: Preaching. | Preaching and ethics. | Christianity and
justice.

Classification: BV4211.3 .M35 2021 (print) | BV4211.3 (ebook)

02/19/21

Contents

Preface

ALTHOUGH I DID NOT start writing this book during the COVID-19 pandemic, I completed it when the pandemic was at its peak. The pandemic revealed anew glaring systemic inequities and inadequacies in health care, elder care, education, labor, and the overall economy. As my writing and editing came to an end, George Floyd was brutally killed by police in Minneapolis and our nation, and the world, began to march in the streets petitioning for long overdue structural changes in policing practices and the criminal justice system. Once again, my white privilege became painfully clear to me as I watched the news and social media daily. As I think about each ethical approach in this book, they now feel more urgent than ever. It is clear that they have the potential to help preachers speak to the many ethical issues unearthed by the pandemic, and by our new commitment to challenging structural racism in the months and years ahead.

This is an unprecedented time of opportunity in our nation and in the world. It should now be much clearer that we cannot rely on our current institutions, ideologies, or many of our theologies to frame adequate solutions for the future. We need more than quick fixes, moral platitudes, and political squabbles. We need bold, imaginative change that can bring us together and improve our ordinary lives. Each of the approaches in this book is focused on an aspect of that task, whether it be establishing a new moral consensus, providing an alternative and countercultural moral vision, educating and enrolling people in revolutionary change, or creating face-to-face relationships that will welcome unheard voices into the process of moral renewal. I believe that if preachers cultivate any or all of these aspects during this opportune time, they can lend tremendous support to the public changes that are needed today.

Acknowledgments

I AM INDEBTED TO Vanderbilt Divinity School, its students, faculty, and Dean Emilie Townes, for embodying in unique and complex ways the range of ethical approaches found in this book. I have taught a course entitled "Ethical Approaches to Preaching" for several years, and my students generated many of the ideas found in this book. Over the years they have helped me refine the lectures that are at the core of each chapter. I have on file many student sermons that represent wonderful examples of each of these ethical approaches and I have fond memories of hearing them preached in class. In conversations with faculty colleagues over the years, and by reading their books and articles, I have discovered a rich treasure trove of theological and ethical thought that has improved my thinking many times over. And it has been a great joy to have a dean who "walks the walk," demonstrating many of the ideas in this book through her priorities and commitments. I am also grateful to Aimee Moiso, who offered me her conceptual and editing genius in the final stages of this project.

When all is said and done it is my homiletical colleagues throughout the world who are to be thanked most of all for the ideas in this book. I am summarizing their thoughts here, and I hope that I have been fair and measured. They have inspired me over and over again during my career, and I have seen my students transformed by interacting with their ideas in classrooms and diverse contexts. Special relationships have marked my way, including but not limited to Chuck Campbell, Ronald Allen, Sally Brown, Dawn Ottoni-Wilhelm, Frank Thomas, Lucy Rose, Kathy Black, Eunjoo Mary Kim, Dale Andrews, Mary Lin Hudson, Christine Smith, and Nora Tubbs Tisdale. In different ways, these scholars have challenged and shaped my thinking in this book. I write this book in their honor, and in honor of all those mentioned in this book that have made such a profound difference in the way preaching is now considered a distinctly ethical practice.

Introduction

CHRISTIAN ETHICISTS BRING CHRISTIAN texts, traditions, and practices into conversation with current ethical resources in order to decide on the best ways to think and act in relation to moral issues. In this process, specific human virtues are identified, ideal forms of human action and interaction are embraced, and visions of justice are projected against the backdrop of human history. Although some argue that ethics and theology are different or even competing modes of reflection, and that ethics is "mere philosophy," this position makes little if any real sense. No matter how interior or transcendent theological ideas may seem, they always harbor implicit or explicit ideas regarding how we ought to live and behave as Christians. These ideas have a long history of influence in the public sphere, and within democratic societies they influence voters and the politicians whom they hold responsible.

The current generation of homileticians (scholars who think about and theorize preaching) has been richly blessed with thinkers who have helped us reflect more deeply on the ethical aspects of preaching. These scholars show us ways to better understand how it is that preaching and sermon-listening are always theo-ethical Christian practices. They treat preaching as an ethical activity of the first order because preaching is concerned with helping congregations, and by extension society itself, catch a glimpse of what is ultimately good and how best to live in this world. Week after week, preachers narrate a theological story that helps people understand what is wrong in the world, and what is required in order to make things more commensurate with God's vision.

My overarching purpose for writing this book is to provide an overview of four kinds of ethics that have been shaped by contemporary scholars into ways to help working preachers approach difficult ethical issues: (1) communicative ethics, (2) witness ethics, (3) liberation ethics, and (4) hospitality ethics. My goal is not to produce a book on Christian ethics, or even a book on homiletical ethics per se, but to summarize and organize in a practical fashion the rich variety of ways that preaching is being construed today as an ethical practice.

The time is right for this kind of resource. Churches and public institutions are mired in ethical conflict and disagreement. Many preachers find themselves in "purple" congregations where politically red and blue parishioners sit together and live in disagreement about many difficult moral issues. Most sermon listeners strive to think more clearly about the intersection of faith and action. They are listening for how their preacher speaks about the impact that faith should have on the way they live, and on the personal, social, and political choices they make.

As preachers, we cannot assume that "one size of preaching fits all." When deciding how to approach an ethical problem, we must consider many things: the moment in history we occupy; the ways our listeners are prone to think; the relational, personal, communal, financial, or social constraints that bind us and our listeners; the kind of preaching our congregation is accustomed to hearing or values most; the social, economic, and geographic location of our congregation; and many other variables. One approach will not work in every situation. Working preachers need help not only in identifying useful approaches, but in deciding which approach is most appropriate in a given situation. I have designed this publication to help preachers make these decisions.

This is a brief introductory handbook. As such, it provides a thumbnail overview of four distinct ethical approaches to preaching. Each chapter identifies the major emphases within each approach, attempting to give a general feel for each approach and what it can best accomplish. Boiling a large body of literature down into four identifiable approaches inevitably means that some of the unique characteristics of the writings of key contributors will get lost. I do believe, however, that the core ideas that guide each cluster of scholars I am distilling are similar, and that I am being faithful to the larger contours of their work. I also focus attention on certain scholars more than others, and no doubt fail to identify every possible scholar at work within each approach. I leave it to those who read or teach these approaches to build additional bridges to writers who are either left out or are only modestly included.

Given the great diversity of preaching styles, readers are likely to experience some anxiety over the idea that preachers or sermons can be neatly slotted into any single category. What about hybrid approaches? Aren't there lots of good reasons to mix together elements of different approaches? Don't some features float between different approaches? These are important questions. For a practice as dynamic and fluid as preaching, creating types, models, categories, or approaches can impose a false sense of order and organization. I have drawn fairly rigid boundaries between these approaches, however, for a pedagogical reason. They are meant to help the reader discover contrasting approaches on their own terms first in order to see as clearly as possible how each approach best functions. I believe that we do not have the luxury of discussing the cross fertilization of approaches until we have learned the actual approaches that currently exist. Once this is accomplished, it is easier to see when and how various hybrid approaches might be created, or how different approaches can effectively inform one another.

There are perspectives on preaching besides the ethical, including but not limited to evangelistic, liturgical, theological, educational, and cultural perspectives. Preaching is multifaceted and cannot be completely defined by one perspective alone. Many intersections between these perspectives have come into view in this book, and I have done my best to highlight these intersections without letting an entirely different emphasis take over our discussion of ethics. I believe that preaching is best learned when we learn it piece by piece—focusing on each aspect in its own right, one at a time. When this is done, we begin to see each perspective more clearly and can make more informed choices about how we want to preach.

What is an Approach?

An approach is something more practical and accessible than a theory. If I were to offer the reader ethical theories of preaching, I would need to provide a fairly extensive intellectual history informing each theory, identifying key epistemological and philosophical assumptions, core methodologies, crucial arguments, and critical questions or issues. These are not unimportant for the task at hand, and I will provide aspects of this information that I deem most important. I anticipate that readers will make good use of the additional reading at the end of each chapter to dig further into these matters as desired. An approach, however, is different from a theory. It is a practical way to get from here to there. Getting from here to there involves developing certain habits, and a specific habitus or "feel for the game." As I have driven from my home to my office each day, I have developed certain habits. I know that if I go one direction at rush hour it will take longer. I need to adjust and go another way. Over the years I've developed a feel for the game of driving to work. I know almost implicitly which approach to my office will get me there in a more expedient fashion and which maps or GPS apps will help me most. The crucial questions, if I want to approach something, are:

- Why leave where I am in the first place?

- What are the main obstacles in my way?

- Who do I need to take with me?

- How do I get them on board?
- How do I get there?
- Which direction should I go?
- What choices should I make?
- What signposts should I look for?
- What should I take with me or leave behind?
- Is there a good map available?
- What tactics or strategies should I employ?
- Where exactly am I going?

In this handbook I boil these down to four questions that help organize the key elements of each approach. As I analyze each approach in each chapter, these questions guide the way:

1. How do preachers theologically frame an ethical problem in order for listeners to identify the best way out of the problem?

2. How do preachers create a personal and communal experience of this problem and the best way into understanding and engaging it constructively?

3. What signposts should the preacher follow in order to organize the best way through the problem or issue?

4. How do preachers articulate a final destination and the best way toward it?

1. The Way Out

Each ethical approach provides a characteristic way of conceptualizing that out-of-which preaching wants to lead sermon listeners or participants. Not only does each approach conceptualize what is wrong (sin, evil, etc.) in a specific way, it suggests a way to respond to these evils and the obstacles they create. Preaching itself becomes a way to engage these things, and to help provide participants a way out. For instance, in one approach the preacher is articulating a way out of the "Domination System," the so-called "principalities and powers," especially demonic systems of privilege, violence, and abusive power. Forms of preaching that embody non-accommodation and resistance provide the best way out of this situation. In another approach, the preacher is articulating a way out of moral insularity, the ways people become siloed within bubbles of preference and prejudice. Only by working hard to get into the shoes of others and increasing empathy for the suffering of others can a way out be found. Preachers who take this approach will embody practices of consensus-seeking across dividing lines in order to find a way out of the moral deadlocks that are destroying our common life. Each approach defines the problem and the way out of that problem differently.

2. The Way In

Ethical approaches to preaching have to provide listeners with a way into the ethical issue at hand. Listeners need to identify with an issue and become invested in it. Each approach must answer such questions as:

- What are the common experiences of the ethical issue?

- Where are my sermon listeners in relation to this issue?

- How can I help us identify with and understand those who have different experiences of this issue?

- How do I motivate people to care about an issue? How can I get sermon listeners on board?

- What kinds of illustrations or other forms of imaginative or actual involvement will help to get us all on the same page?

- What are the shared pathways into a particular ethical issue?

- What kinds of authentic sermonic engagement will give most people a way into the kinds of action that might make a difference?

Every homiletical approach has to provide a way into an ethical journey, provoking real life connections that will make an ethical problem and a particular direction of thinking and acting important to listeners. This can include such things as illustrations, analogies, stories, identifications, imagery, or clarifications of various types.

3. The Way Through

Each ethical approach to preaching must provide cognitive and affective signposts (key concepts, symbols, messages, categories of thought, topics, tropes, feelings) so that listeners know where they are and what is at stake as a particular ethical terrain is crossed:

- What issues or roadblocks need to be dealt with?

- What themes require treatment?

- What theological categories are likely to be most helpful for preaching about this issue?

- What feeling tones should sermons have?

- What memorable terms or phrases will help people grasp where we are in our ethical journey and what the most important landmarks are?

- What communication strategies are best?

Each homiletical approach makes use of a distinct way of messaging and of organizing thoughts, ideas, and feelings so that people know where they are and what aspect of an ethical norm or issue is under discussion. Some forms of messaging will be more artistic and imaginative. Others will be relatively didactic or catechetical. Some will be more visual or even theatrical. Others will be more conversational and measured. Some will move from problem to solution. Others will move from lamentation to hope. Each homiletical approach organizes a specific way through a particular ethical terrain.

4. The Way Toward

Each ethical approach to preaching carries within it a recognizable eschatology. Even as each approach identifies "What is wrong?" and "Why?" (the way out), each approach also identifies "What does it mean to be a person of faith?" "Do I have any help?" "Where are we going?" (the way toward). The ethical approaches in this book tell this narrative in different ways, depicting an exemplary vision of a hoped-for future. No matter which approach is used, preachers will identify and claim a way toward a new and better world.

Getting the Feel for Each Approach

When I first moved to Nashville a neighbor told me about the three best ways to get to my office. I didn't really get the feel for driving to work, however, until he drove me to and from my office several times, rehearsing the reasons why each approach was preferable at different times of the day. In much the same way, learning about an approach to preaching is different from seeing it in action. How do the four elements of each approach contribute to the way an ethical issue is actually preached? How can I get the feel for each approach? What does each kind of sermon look like, or sound like? What do these approaches look like in action? To answer these questions, I will act as your tour guide. I have written a sample topical sermon for each approach. To accentuate the differences between approaches, I have used the same topic for all four sermons: immigration. This will help the reader experience the uniqueness of each ethical approach when applied to the same moral issue. These sermons are intentionally crafted to emphasize some of the key features of each ethical approach, and to clarify what the approach looks and sounds like. I have also included a few annotations in the margins that draw attention to features of the approach that are important to notice.

Determining the Best Approach

As practicing preachers, we are committed already to certain ways of getting things done. This often means, however, that we become locked into one strategy in a one-size-fits-all way. In some instances, this works fairly well. In others, not so well. Determining the best approach for a particular situation and adjusting our practice requires vocational and situational reflection. We need to take a good hard look at our usual ways of preaching and bring those into conversation with the reality of the larger context, our immediate situation, and the expectations that push and pull at us from all sides. In short, we have to become reflective practitioners and practical theologians, reading situations, and becoming aware of the assumptions and expectations of those who will hear or overhear our sermons. This reflection helps us decide what approach will work best in the here and now, in this place and time.

Essentially, I will be asking preachers to determine what they really need in their specific situation and inviting them to choose the best ethical approach to preaching to meet that situation. If they see their work as that of doing public theology, translating the gospel into street-level language and helping to establish a new moral consensus, then I invite them to consider a communicative ethic. If they believe that their situation requires the development of churches or organizations of distinctly Christian character that are willing to testify boldly on behalf of a countercultural, nonviolent moral vision, then I encourage them to consider a witness ethic. If preachers believe that their congregation needs to be reeducated about white supremacy, poverty, the criminal justice system, and other systems of injustice, and become better organized to join with other social movements for revolutionary change, then I suggest engaging a liberationist ethic. If the preacher's situation is one where people need to cultivate moral relationships, by coming face to face and talking, learning how to listen, speak, and work together morally in spite of their differences, then I invite them to adopt an ethic of hospitality.

In order to help preachers understand the kinds of contexts and situations that are best suited for each approach, I provide two things. First, near the end of each chapter, I offer a brief section that makes suggestions regarding the kinds of situations that call for each approach. This is not meant to be exhaustive, but to help steer preachers in the best homiletical direction given their particular circumstances. Second, in order to clarify how each approach actually functions in particular historical contexts and situations, I provide a situational sermon example by a preacher who in my estimation exemplifies how the approach has been put to good use in a particular time and place. Observing thoughtful preachers at work in specific historical and social contexts can teach us many things about what it means to function as practical theologians and ethicists in particular situations.

The Importance of Further Reading

Several preachers and scholars have shaped each approach outlined in this handbook. While I have culled much of their wisdom and made it as accessible as possible, further reading will lead to the discovery of important additional insights, theoretical formulations, examples, and ideas for application and practice. I strongly encourage reading into the larger body of literature that is available. In order to get this reading started, I have included a list of "additional reading" at the end of each chapter.

A Roadmap

To summarize, in four chapters I identify four ethical approaches to preaching: (1) a communicative ethic, (2) a witness ethic, (3) a liberation ethic, and (4) an ethic of hospitality. In each chapter I work through four core questions and identify: (1) the way out, (2) the way in, (3) the way through, and (4) the way toward. Next, I include an annotated sermon example that I have crafted in order to help further clarify the approach. I then offer a brief section highlighting the kinds of situations that call for the ethical approach, followed by a contextual sermon example that shows the approach at work. Finally, I provide a short list of additional reading. A more extensive bibliography can be found at the end of the book.

1

Communicative Ethics

COMMUNICATIVE ETHICS IS A mode of procedural ethics focused on identifying the best intersubjective process for achieving moral consensus.[1] Although German philosopher and sociologist Jürgen Habermas is often credited with shaping this ethical approach, it has a long parallel history within communication theory, the development of democratic practices, debate, rules of order (such as Robert's Rules), and theories of conflict resolution and transformation. Communicative ethicists are pragmatists. They are looking for moral norms that will work for as many people as possible, across all conceivable lines of difference.

A communicative ethic is an *intersubjective* ethic. It relies on determining and understanding the best arguments put forward by groups of people who occupy clear subject positions within the social order. For the communicative ethicist, the propositions and proposals that are debated must be rational and publicly verifiable. Moral discourse can only be conducted among and by those who are self-reflective social actors—those who see themselves as carving out and living into certain positions on ethical issues that are publicly identifiable and rationally defensible.

1. For more on procedural ethics see Habermas, "Morality and Ethical Life."

Communicative ethics is focused on searching for and applying *universally* acceptable moral norms. Because of this, when preachers adopt this approach, their understanding of their audience must expand dramatically. The congregation extends far beyond the people sitting in the pews on Sunday morning. Preachers who are communicative ethicists envision their congregation as public and, at least theoretically, universal in scope. The ultimate goal for the communicative ethicist in the pulpit is to articulate moral norms that can be considered, at least for the time being, as right for as many people as possible.[2] This requires a journey beyond the preacher's and congregation's own relatively small world and into other social locations, situations, and lifestyles. The preacher must be broadly consultative and empathic, asking what might be right for persons occupying widely divergent subject positions: different political parties, distinct geographic regions, diverse racial and ethnic backgrounds, various cultures and subcultures, differing gender identities, and contrasting abilities and disabilities. Because broad moral consensus is sought, preachers who adopt this approach to ethics take it upon themselves to read widely, listen carefully to public debates, and consult others who are significantly impacted by particular ethical issues.

A communicative ethic preacher draws intellectual resources from religionists and modern liberal and social gospel theologians. These scholars often accentuate common underlying religious experiences that religious traditions express in different ways and seek to re-approach through Scriptures, ritual practices, and doctrinal writings. They identify a range of these experiences, such as an experience of the holy or *mysterium fascinans et tremendum* (Rudolf Otto), absolute dependence (Fredrich Schleiermacher), or being grasped by ultimate concern (Paul Tillich).[3] Social gospel theologian Walter Rauschenbusch identified the idea of the reign

---

2. Normative "rightness" is a crucial "validity claim" in Habermas's communicative ethic and is a function of the broadest possible "role-taking" across all kinds of subject positions. See Habermas, *On the Pragmatics of Social Interaction*, 92.

3. Schleiermacher, *The Christian Faith*, 16–17; Otto, *The Idea of the Holy*, 12–40; Tillich, *Dynamics of Faith*, 1–30.

of God—a time of justice and peace as the realizable and ultimate goal of history—as the universal principle at the heart of Christianity, overlapping in many ways with ethical visions within other religions. According to Rauschenbusch, this reign of God will be a community of righteousness "which will guarantee to all personalities their freest and highest development" and will inaugurate "a progressive reign of love in human affairs."[4] More recently, Helene Slessarev-Jamir, in her book *Prophetic Activism*, looks at several major world religions and identifies an ethical core idea that she calls the "prophetic" or "the sacred and reciprocal quality of all human life, out of which flow(s) a call to do justice to the *other*."[5] Similar to these scholars, communicative ethicists go in search of universal religious and moral experiences and strive to translate them into expressive, contemporary, and accessible language.

Perhaps the best example in the North American context of this universalist kind of ethical preaching is the preaching of Martin Luther King, Jr., who never gave up trying to reach across all of the lines of difference around him. When he spoke, he worked hard to find genuine moral norms that *as many people as possible* could understand and make their own. He appealed to large concepts such as human dignity, human rights, individual freedom, mercy, love, and hope. He attempted to articulate places of common (and high) ethical ground that exist between all morally conscious human beings across all situations, contexts, and cultures. Although many of these moral norms had significant roots in King's Christian religious tradition and in its Scriptures, they were also norms that might be shared across many world religions, as well as across different philosophical and political worldviews.

The goal of *communication* for the communicative ethicist is an experience of binding/bonding—of universal empathic understanding. Similar to communion, communication represents a coming together, a sharing in something, a consubstantiality in the reality of ethical discernment and understanding. Communicative ethicists believe that people would not even speak together at all

4. Rauschenbusch, *Theology for the Social Gospel*, 142.

5. Slessarev-Jamir, *Prophetic Activism*, 5.

if they did not believe that they could find some kind of common ground or new plateau of understanding between them. Although efforts at communication can go awry and conflict or disagreement remain, the very effort itself, when it is genuine, has a redemptive element within it. There can be a certain kind of binding/bonding in that experience—the experience of genuine communicative discernment, in which every stakeholder who can participate is allowed to take part, everyone is permitted to ask questions, everyone is able to put forward proposals, everyone can express where they are coming from, what they want, and what they need, and the aim of communication remains intact.

The Way Out

For the preacher as communicative ethicist, two fundamental problems must be addressed when approaching any ethical issue: (1) *insincerity,* or the inability or unwillingness to be truthful, and (2) *insularity*, or the inability or unwillingness to take the perspective of others or "role-take."[6]

Confronting Insincerity

First of all, communicative ethic preachers help sermon listeners confront common forms of insincerity or untruthfulness. It is important for those who engage in moral arguments to be as truthful as possible. Ethical communicators should not harbor vindictive, vain, cynical, self-serving, malicious, narcissistic, devious, harmful, or potentially violent motives. Participants in moral debate require a significant amount of self-knowledge regarding their social locations, interests, privileges, attitudes, ideological biases, blind spots, pathologies, and previous mistakes. There can be no openness to other positions without humility and self-awareness about the nature and limitations of one's own.

6. See Mead, *Mind, Self, and Society*, 154–64.

The Christian faith provides a crucial liturgical practice that is significant for overcoming untruthfulness and insincerity: confession/conversion. When Christians confess their sin, they are saying to themselves and to others:

- I don't know it all.

- I haven't always gotten things right.

- The commitments that I have been holding might be wrong and need changing.

- I can be self-deceived, and I need to work at that!

- I can be converted from my current way of thinking and acting.

- I can change.

Confessional practices, if they are taken seriously and given traction in one's moral deliberations, help to assure truthfulness in conversations in which universal moral norms are being pursued. In essence, confession can keep participants in difficult moral conversations from becoming deceived by self-interest or by tragic over-commitment to an assumed ideological position. Participants practice humility about assumptions, ideologies, and forms of self-interest. This increases the possibility and likelihood of *converting* from hard-and-fast ideological, personal, or prejudicial positions. Humility and openness to changing one's mind are crucial if we are to find a way out of the current moral situation toward new ground.

Christian practices of confession also allow for the bracketing of the voices of those who have been proven to intend violence or harm to participants in a moral debate. The early church instituted a tiered practice of confession called *exomologesis* (meaning "out of unity") whereby those known to intend evil or violence could be excluded from the community and its moral discourse. Although in some cases these persons could repent and be welcomed back under strict cautionary procedures, in many instances they were not permitted to participate and became recipients primarily of the intercession of churchgoers.

In worst case situations where moral debate is underway, this might mean excluding the arguments of those who have unrepentant and verifiably unaltered histories of violence, falsehood, divisive faking of information (as in fake news), abuse, or prejudice. This is especially required when such persons intend immediate harm to key interlocutors in a particular ethical conversation. For instance, many were concerned that Jeff Sessions should not be involved in ethical conversations regarding race relations and voter rights, given his unrepentant past record during the civil rights movement in the state of Alabama. Similar ethical questions were raised about Supreme Court Judge Kavanaugh and Senator Al Franken. Many were concerned that, given possible blind spots regarding women's rights in relation to their own bodies, and non-self-reflective attitudes the men displayed regarding these possibilities, they should not be involved in conversations about moral issues pertaining to women's choices. In both of these instances, the central issue was whether or not each of these individuals had adequate *self-knowledge* to transcend their own blind spots, previous mistakes, and prejudices so that they could enter certain ethical conversations as *truthful (non-self-deceived)* participants.

Confronting Insularity

Second, communicative ethic preachers are committed to finding a way out of the human inclination toward insularity of thought and action. When preachers and congregations become insulated from other points of view, unable or unwilling to attend to moral arguments from those occupying other subject positions (ideologies, social locations, religious commitments, races, genders, etc.), they can lose a sense of the broader values, commitments, and purposes they might share with the larger world. They are prone to give up on the possibility of any sort of ethical binding/bonding experience beyond the parochial experiences of congregational life and worship.

For preachers, confronting insularity requires helping their listeners consult other social perspectives than their own. Social psychologists such as George Herbert Mead and John Flavell call this "role-taking," or getting into the shoes of others.[7] While engaging in direct face-to-face biblical, theological, and cultural interpretation is not required (see hospitality ethic in chapter 4), preachers need to study carefully what it is like to occupy the social situations that influence other perspectives on an ethical issue. This concern for adequate role-taking informs most liberal democratic ways of thinking. Without communication across the aisle and beyond, there can be no true democratic process.

For the communicative ethicist, Christian ethical practice often means leaving the church entirely and venturing into town hall spaces where moral deliberations and debate are taking place. It means reaching across religious and political lines. This might involve visiting mosques and synagogues and inviting persons of other religions and faiths to come together in local churches. It might mean holding town hall forums at church, where political or social leaders debate and discuss difficult ethical issues and the people they believe they are representing. It might mean that members of the church attend together public meetings on fair housing, fair wages, and fair employment, while also listening to local residents, developers, bankers, and members of the Better Business Bureau. It could mean that Sunday school classes will invite the best environmentalists one week, and climate skeptics the next. It will mean listening carefully to persons who do not share our racial or ethnic backgrounds, or who attend different schools (or none at all). It involves hearing from those who have differing perspectives on the abortion debate, the immigration debate, the welfare debate, the euthanasia debate, and other issues. This does not mean that we hear from everyone who dreams up a theory or idea about a moral issue. It is important to remember that those involved in these conversations need to

7. Mead, *Mind, Self, and Society*, 153–64. Flavell, *The Development of Role-Taking*.

be working hard at non-self-deception and sincerely seeking to understand and learn together.

Communicative ethic preachers will urge road trips to visit persons in rural or urban situations that diverge from the congregation's usual experience. They will encourage holding conversations about sacred texts that we do not share (the Talmud, the Quran, the Vedas, the Book of Mormon, etc.), and about quasi-sacred texts that we do share: The Constitution, The Bill of Rights, the *Roe vs. Wade* ruling, or The Dream Act. With regard to ethical issues, the preacher's congregation often becomes a religiously attenuated public forum within a larger public forum.

Another important liturgical practice helps the communicative ethicist learn role-taking skills: *intercession*. As Christians, the practice of intercession teaches participants to get into the shoes of others (role-take). Intercessors role-take with a particular eye to human *suffering*. On Sunday morning many churches offer "prayers of the people" or pastoral prayers during which participants work hard to identify with the suffering around the world. During such prayers, they go beyond merely empathizing with suffering persons. They become advocates, offering up specific petitions on behalf of others. In some situations, as they are able, intercessors even pray for enemies or those who may persecute them or wish them harm. This can be crucial for communicative ethics. If a liberal urban Democrat can go to those places where the rural red state Republican is actually suffering, and then pray for him/her, it creates a much better chance of finding plateaus of common ground and understanding. The same is true if we run this the other direction.

To summarize, for the communicative ethicist in the pulpit, the core problem is that ethical issues can be treated in ways that are insincere and insular, bounded by high walls of self-deception and prejudice, and non-consultative of the many contrasting perspectives that are possible on ideas, themes, and moral issues. The way out, therefore, is through sincere, truthful (non-self-deceived), and empathic consultation of many interpretations and perspectives across anticipated lines of difference.

The Way In

As mentioned above, for the communicative ethic preacher the congregation consists not only of the people sitting in the pews on Sunday morning, but of the larger public arena we inhabit. In such a homiletical situation, how does the preacher find a way into all of those diverse contexts and lives? Are not the Christian faith and the biblical texts from which it is derived quite distant and strange? In this situation, preachers need to do several things to provide a way into a moral issue: translating biblical and theological language, providing public moral exemplars, and using illustrations to elucidate moral disagreements, possibilities, and ongoing struggles.

Translating Biblical and Theological Language

Because they want to be always in conversation with a larger public beyond their congregation, it is incumbent on the preacher as communicative ethicist to translate difficult-to-understand biblical and theological categories into terms that make sense for those who are not necessarily Christians. This does not mean sacrificing all of the particularity of an idea, which will have many layers of textured meaning for the believer. It means finding new language in the same way that a good Bible paraphraser is able to do (cf. Eugene Peterson's *The Message*), only with a specific ethical conversation in mind. This means breaking biblical language down into the vernacular of an ethical discussion.

Another translation strategy is to think metaphorically. Metaphors are created by juxtaposing a more abstract word or idea with a more concrete one (for instance: "love is a rose"). When these terms (love/rose) are juxtaposed, a surplus of meaning occurs between the two terms whereby each term invites the other one to learn something. When Martin Luther King, Jr. juxtaposed language from the exodus narrative in the Bible with the African American experience in his "I've been to the mountaintop" speech, he was using both terms to translate each other in a way that could provoke a surplus of meaning and provide secularists,

Christians, and persons of other faiths a way to mutually translate one another's experiences. Both Rudolf Bultmann and Paul Tillich were champions of this kind of thinking. In their generation, for instance, "salvation" was translated as "authentic existence" (Bultmann) and "the courage to be" (Tillich). Authenticity in a world of inauthenticity, and the courage to be in the face of a world bent on non-being and self-destruction became useful ways to translate an arcane theological category into language that might make better sense in the public realm. For the communicative ethicist in the pulpit this kind of translation is crucial and often requires some imaginative work. People have to develop what Frank Thomas calls a "moral imagination" wherein biblical categories are re-imagined in relationship to the moral issues of our day.[8]

Identifying Public Exemplars

Sermon illustrations often provide a good way into an ethical issue by helping listeners identify with persons affected by a moral issue. When the communicative ethic preacher wants to illustrate what they are saying, they do not focus on providing images or stories about individuals in their congregation or in the church. Christian exemplars, or people who are "like us" in some pejorative fashion, are not central to these illustrations. Instead, illustrations will most often come from the larger culture or public arena. Using what H. Richard Niebuhr called a "Christ of Culture" approach, preachers easily find exemplars for the things they are talking about among those who are not necessarily religious persons at all, but who will be widely known by sermon listeners. These exemplars do not have to come from within the immediate situation but may be retrieved from history or projected onto the screen of the future in an imaginative fashion. Martin Luther King, Jr. did this, for instance, when he imagined black and white children playing together and living in harmony. It does not matter whether these were "church" children at all. The fact that they are playing together in equity

8. Thomas, *How to Preach a Dangerous Sermon.*

and harmony provides a way in to a new moral norm for all of
King's listeners, and while also illustrating the "gospel" for those
Christians with ears to hear.

Using Illustrations to Elucidate

Elucidation means "telling it like it is." For the communicative
ethicist, illustrations are designed to help listeners see into the
actual world shaped by a moral issue in all of its stark reality.
The goal is to help listeners experience what rings false and what
rings true within a moral debate or conversation. This can take
several shapes. First, illustrations can elucidate ethical disagreement. In this aspect, illustrations show us pictures of moral
disruption, trouble, or conflict, and indicate a dissensus in our
midst. Preachers go in search of larger, cultural pictures of how
our moral understanding is flawed, and show the genuine moral
conundrum we face together. For instance, this might involve offering a picture of someone living with difficulty, and perhaps
even suffering under current moral norms and legislation: a
migrant dreamer being deported, a gay couple struggling to get
a marriage license, an African American voter experiencing obstacles at the polls on Election Day.

Second, illustrations can elucidate by revealing new possibilities for people's lives in relationship to a moral issue—people
who might be seen as "ahead of the game" in terms of what they
represent. For instance, in relation to the debate on same-sex
marriage, the preacher might paint a portrait of a same-sex marriage where children in the family are flourishing. Or in relation
to the immigration issue, the preacher might paint a portrait of a
migrant family making a unique and unparalleled contribution to
a neighborhood or community. The lives of such persons embody
new possibilities or moral insights that anticipate a new public
consensus. They become "gospel-pictures" inasmuch as they
show us the good news of what life might be like given a new,
lived situation in relation to a moral issue.

Finally, illustrations might show us pictures of persons or groups *struggling* within their own historical circumstances to accommodate to existing moral norms or to a new moral norm that changes their lives in some way. The preacher shows pictures of how complex it can be to struggle with moral norms, whether old or new. This helps us recognize our own lives in the big picture of a moral debate, or a new moral solution. For instance, the preacher might offer realistic pictures of how certain immigration laws, when passed, create new struggles in local communities, congregations, and among nations. Real adjustments have to occur. Such examples provide a way into the complexity of all moral legislation and keep empathy and role-taking alive and moving forward.

The Way Through

Three typical characteristics stand out in the way that communicative ethic preachers create and organize messages and provide signposts through difficult ethical terrain: organizing sermons in a problem/solution format, identifying moral norms that work at a broad, universal level, and demonstrating the importance of good moral judgment.

Preaching Moral Problems in Search of Solutions

Instead of leading off with biblical and exegetical exposition, these sermons are usually thematic and "problem/solution" driven. From the outset an ethical issue or problem is on the table for deliberation, and the sermon seeks some clarity and ethical understanding. Because an ethical conundrum is being sorted out, sermons will often take the shape of puzzles in pursuit of new insights or resolutions. Often, the biblical text is used to provoke this puzzle, or to open up an issue that needs to be addressed. The text "troubles the waters" of the way an ethical issue has been framed. The Bible is treated in a *Midrashic* fashion, raising new questions, pushing a moral issue into the foreground, creating cognitive conflict where none exists, issuing a new provocation. The sermon deepens this problem and explores some of its aspects in a way that engages diverse perspectives. Then, if possible, some sort of insight or (partial) resolution comes into view by the end of the sermon. This could be as simple as identifying a new direction of thought, a new possibility, a convergence of opinion, or a working hypothesis.

Identifying Thin Moral Norms

The communicative ethicist is looking for potentially *universal* norms. This means that new working hypotheses have to be tested against an enormous range of human experience. The preacher has to be clear that what is being sought is something that will work in the public sphere, and such things may not be fully satisfactory within particular doctrinally motivated religious communities. This usually means that preachers will go in search of moral norms that are more general or *thin*.[9] Thin norms are not bound to singular ideologies or traditions and operate at a higher level of abstraction. Thick ethical norms are voiced exclusively in the unique language and categories of thought within particular religious or ideological traditions. For the communicative ethicist thick norms will be used in a supportive role only. Preachers will search out moral norms that can operate at a higher level of abstraction (are broader and more general in nature) in order to be acceptable for more people. A good example of ethically thick and thin treatments of a moral issue occurred after the terrorist attack on the World Trade Towers and Pentagon. Pat Robertson and Jerry Falwell both preached a similar jeremiad as their moral argument: God allowed this to happen to America because of its immorality, seen especially in its emerging stances on human rights and homosexuality. The moral norm at stake was the requirement to please God by returning to proper conservative forms of social and sexual behavior. This argument reflected an exclusive, biblically

9. For more on "thin" and "thick" moral norms see Miller, *Terror, Religion, and Liberal Thought*, 122, 124. See also Lloyd, "Thick or Thin?"

and theologically thick moral dictum that would appeal mostly to a narrow audience representative of a cluster of intersecting ideological paradigms, such as evangelical Christianity, American exceptionalism, and heteronormativity. On the other hand, in his now famous sermon Jeremiah Wright went to a thinner place morally. He chose Psalm 137 as his text, a psalm ostensibly about revenge by people who have watched their loved ones die. He notices how easy it would be to allow the desire for revenge to become a desire for "paybacks" at any cost—even at the cost of *innocent* lives. He chooses, therefore, to argue for a thin moral norm that might work across many paradigms of moral thinking: *killing ordinary citizens as they go about their day-to-day lives is wrong.* Ostensibly, persons of many religions, political parties, and ideological perspectives could agree with this norm. Of course, ethical norms such as this can also be argued within the thickness of the biblical narrative and the doctrinal concepts, ideas, and propositions that derive from that narrative. Ultimately, however, these concepts have to be translated into to a thin enough moral proposition to function within the public sphere across many different communities of moral discourse.

Demonstrating the Importance of Good Theological Judgment

For the communicative ethicist, good judgment is crucial. Cardinal John Henry Newman once called this quality of religious leadership the "illative sense," by which he meant a sense for deciding what idea or thought is best to apply in a given situation.[10] For the communicative ethicist, this involves deciding what might reach the largest range of persons implicated. We see this kind of good judgment in Jeremiah Wright's sermon, noted above. He speaks in the sermon about how difficult that decision was—deciding what to say, and how to say it. In the end, he decided to preach an idea that would provide moral vision to the largest public possible,

10. See McClure, "In Pursuit of Good Theological Judgment."

including Christians, Muslims, and persons of other religions, as well as agnostics and secularists. This is perhaps the most important way communicative ethicists provide a path through moral dilemmas and crises. They step back from the situation and attempt to gain enough distance to make an appropriate judgment about the most universally acceptable moral norm for the situation at hand. This is difficult and requires a certain amount of experience and wisdom to do well.

These decisions are often theological in nature. The preacher must assess which theological category is most applicable. In relation to the gay rights debate, for instance, if the preacher decides that homosexuality should be slotted into the category of "sin," this promotes a different translation in the public domain (dysfunction? deviancy? abnormality?) from the preacher who makes the judgment to slot homosexuality into the theological category of "creation," which would translate very differently (DNA? molecular biology?). As a communicative ethicist, one's judgment about theological framing and application will be crucial for providing signposts through difficult conversations. Demonstrating this kind of judgment suggests to sermon listeners that careful judgment is crucial for all moral deliberations.

The Way Toward

Communicative ethics is utopian in nature. It assumes that a communicative "binding/bonding" telos exists and is embedded within every human interaction. We would not talk with each other at all if we did not want to arrive at some understanding or way to live together and remain in solidarity. Those with a more pessimistic view of human interaction argue that this is at best unrealistic, and at worst delusional. Communicative ethicists in the pulpit and beyond, however, persist in their belief that together we can identify and articulate meaningful thin norms for behavior that, while not necessarily perfectly fitting all worldviews, can in fact bind and bond us together in this world. The vision projected by a communicative ethicist, therefore, is one where mutual respect, desire for the freedom and flourishing of all people, and dialogical participation in shaping moral legislation and social reality are possible. In this larger picture, preachers occupy privileged places of leadership, rhetorical invention, and moral imagination.

Topical Sermon Example: Communicative Ethics

Genesis 11:1–9

¹ Now the whole earth had one language and the same words. ² And as they migrated from the east, they came upon a plain in the land of Shinar and settled there. ³ And they said to one another, "Come, let us make bricks, and burn them thoroughly." And they had brick for stone, and bitumen for mortar. ⁴ Then they said, "Come, let us build ourselves a city, and a tower with its top in the heavens, and let us make a name for ourselves; otherwise we shall be scattered abroad upon the face of the whole earth." ⁵ The LORD came down to see the city and the tower, which mortals had built. ⁶ And the LORD said, "Look, they are one people, and they have all one language; and this is only the beginning of what they will do; nothing that they propose to do will now be impossible for them. ⁷ Come, let us go down, and confuse their language there, so that they will not understand one another's speech." ⁸ So the LORD scattered them abroad from there over the face of all the earth, and they left off building the city. ⁹ Therefore it was called Babel, because there the LORD confused the language of all the earth; and from there the LORD scattered them abroad over the face of all the earth.

Acts 2:1–13

¹ When the day of Pentecost had come, they were all together in one place. ² And suddenly from heaven there came a sound like the rush of a violent wind, and it filled the entire house where they were sitting. ³ Divided tongues, as of fire, appeared among them, and a tongue rested on each of them. ⁴ All of them were filled with the Holy Spirit and began to speak in other languages, as the Spirit gave them ability. ⁵ Now there were devout Jews from every nation under heaven living in Jerusalem. ⁶ And at this sound the crowd gathered and was bewildered, because each one heard them speaking in the native language of each. ⁷ Amazed and astonished, they asked, "Are not all these who are speaking Galileans? ⁸ And how is it that we hear, each of us, in our own native language? ⁹ Parthians, Medes, Elamites, and residents of Mesopotamia, Judea and Cappadocia, Pontus and Asia, ¹⁰ Phrygia and Pamphylia, Egypt and the parts of Libya belonging to Cyrene, and visitors from Rome, both Jews and proselytes, ¹¹ Cretans and Arabs—in our own languages we hear them speaking about God's deeds of power." ¹² All were amazed and perplexed, saying to one another, "What does this mean?" ¹³ But others sneered and said, "They are filled with new wine."

Where Do We Belong?

John S. McClure

My topic this morning is immigration, and I will get to that topic in bits and pieces, however, because I believe that topic is part of a larger moral vision of how we *belong* to one another and to God in this world.

> Instead of beginning with scriptural exposition, notice the thematic and organizational guidance.

To be surrounded by others who speak our language, who talk and think and dress and act and look like us, is comforting. It affirms our natural sense of belonging in this world. It mirrors the way that different species of animals tend to stick together, though of course this is more a social and cultural reality for human beings. And for many of us, it is a religious and political reality as well. It is there in our selection of Facebook friends and groups, in the churches we

> The goal here is to establish a common, "natural" or shared reality where our social, political, and religious belonging is central.

17

choose to attend, in the good friends we spend most of our time with, and even in our choice of which family members are included in which emails or message groups. In the 2008 book *The Big Sort*, Bill Bishop showed that while Americans used to move mainly for individual reasons like higher-paid jobs, nicer weather, and better homes, today they also prioritize living near people who think like they do.[11]

And social belonging is more than a matter of making rational preferential choices. Belonging is also profoundly emotional and affective in nature. We feel when our spaces of personal belonging are safe and thriving, and when they are being invaded and broken apart. Television series and movies play constantly with our sense that certain people belong in one group, and other people belong in another group. The stairs in *Downton Abbey* signify such spaces of belonging—upstairs for the noble folk, downstairs for the common folk—and the plot plays on our emotions as we see people of one class invading the sacred spaces of another class. Terrorist and hostage films such as *Die Hard* and *John Wick* are built largely around our fears that people can be forced, sometimes bodily and violently, out of their safe wombs of belonging and transported into the great chaos of a world where people are trafficked and traded—ripped right out of their places of work or their homes and into the great abyss of global, transnational lawlessness and immorality.

The people on the Plain of Shinar, whose story is told in Genesis 11:1–9, were wrestling with a new sense of belonging. The Table of Nations in Genesis 10 shows how, after the time of Noah's flood, the human family was split into many different ethnic groups and nations. It may seem odd, then, that as Genesis 11 begins, all of these various people around the world speak one language. They "understand" each other. And when they settle in Shinar, which is another name for Babylon, they want to seize hold of one of the greatest powers inherent in such a common language and understanding

We get to the biblical text once the topic and theme are well established.

11. Bishop, *The Big Sort*.

—they want to "make a name" for themselves. In my mind's eye, I see them affixing that name onto the large tower they are building, a ziggurat or building that is wide at the base with increasingly smaller stories reaching into the sky. The story suggests that this use of language and naming exists as a kind of "fortress mentality." In the words of Walter Brueggemann, the people on the Plain of Shinar are seeking "to construct a world free of the danger of the holy, immune from the terrors of God in history . . . a unity grounded in fear and characterized by coercion."[12]

Here we stumble upon a tragic aspect of our natural desire for belonging. Our fear of *not* belonging can encourage us to make a god out of our sameness, and when we do this, we trap God inside of that sameness and singularity. There seems to be something inherently terrifying about not being understood, not

> Notice that sin is not a form of willful disobedience but is tragic in nature—something that cannot be helped and is a consequence of our natural desire for belonging.

belonging, being outside the group, even if just a little bit. And so we build the boundaries tighter. We unfriend others. We build larger walls, larger detention centers, larger prisons. We criminalize more and more people who fall outside the sameness we desire.

An article on the *Psychology Today* blog in 2017 observed that many hardline conservatives share the same personality trait: Social Dominance Orientation (SDO), which refers to people who have preference for the social hierarchy of groups, specifically with a structure in which high-status groups have dominance over low-status groups.[13] As I read about this trait, it seemed to me that it is also shared by hardline progressives. For progressives, high-status groups tend to be more highly educated and cosmopolitan,

> The goal is to see sin as shared across party lines. The communicative ethicist generally avoids taking sides, but wants to show how limitations within all sides potentially inhibit our ability to communicate or find a place of binding/bonding.

whereas for conservatives, high-status groups tend to be defined

---

12. Brueggemann, *Interpretation: Genesis*, 100.

13. Azarian, "An Analysis of Trump Supporters."

by race, ancestry, or regional affiliation. In either case, God is called upon to protect and reinforce the particular form of social dominance which, of course, occurs at the expense of others. We hear stories on both sides of this equation.

Stacey Abrams, former 2018 gubernatorial candidate in Georgia, tells the story about how she, as a high school valedictorian in Georgia, was invited to the governor's mansion along with her peers from other schools. "Everyone was driving up and we were the only ones walking," she says. "When we got to the guard at the gate, he took one look at me and said, 'This is a private event. You don't belong here.'" She went on to say: "I can see he's telling himself a story about me, and I don't know if it's a story about the fact that I'm a young black woman who's walking on the sidewalk, or because he thinks that only poor people ride the bus." As she recalled the story, she said, "I cannot remember meeting the governor of Georgia. I don't remember meeting my colleagues from around the state . . . . All I remember was this man standing in front of the most powerful place in the state and telling me I don't belong."[14]

> This is a story of racial social dominance.

Or there is the story of Sheela Clary, a well-educated liberal, who had a shocking self-realization as she watched college-educated comedian Jordan Klepper, a correspondent on *The Daily Show*, walking through a crowd of Trump supporters mocking their lack of education. In her response, she wrote, "Go pick on someone your own status. Satire should challenge us, not implicate us in taking candy from a baby, or dignity from a kid who might not have much to spare. . . . They might be ignorant, but they are not insane. What are we if we keep getting our cheap laughs the same way, over and over and over again?"[15]

> This is a story of class social dominance.

Social dominance orientation, then, runs all kinds of different ways. And I believe that this is part of what God is displeased with

14. Samuels, "No Place for Hate."
15. Clary, "Smug, Mean, and Contemptuous."

while watching the people on the Plain of Shinar climbing up on their tower built to honor themselves, and engraving their name upon it. God's response is straightforward, but it is not simple. God "scatters" the people. But when God scatters them God says, "Come, let us go down and confuse their language there, so that they will not understand one another's speech" (v. 7).

The goal here is to bring about a confession of the limitations of one's framework or narrative—in order to bring more "truthfulness" to bear in communication.

Here's what I think this is about. God has observed the people on the Plain of Shinar, digging deeper and deeper into their common language, "understanding" each other implicitly, and developing a form of understanding that has a kind of tacit insider and fortress mentality behind it, that invites a knowing wink, or that contains an understanding that "You and I know what we're talking about, don't we?" This is the coded understanding of an in-group. And God wants to "confuse" that kind of understanding, to "scatter" it and break it apart.

Here, the issue of insular language and communication becomes central.

And I believe that this is done on behalf of one thing that is sorely lacking *then*, as well as *now*, and that is *listening*. The Bible is full of stories in which people are speaking, but they are not listening. Joseph's brothers didn't listen to him. Jeremiah complains that for twenty-three years the Judeans failed to listen to him. And if you notice, it is listening and hearing that is central to the story of Pentecost in Acts 2, which is paired with this story from Genesis in the Common Lectionary.

The goal here is to appeal for more profound forms of role-taking and empathy—an intercessory appeal.

". . . each one *heard* them speaking in his own language" (v. 6).

"How is it that we *hear* each one of us in his own native language?" (v.8).

21

"We *hear* them telling in our own tongues the mighty works of God" (v.11).

"Give *ear* to my words" (v. 14).

"Now when they *heard* this they were cut to the heart" (v. 37).

God wants silence and listening, not speaking and "understanding." God wants us to learn how to be silent and listen because that is the only way that we can ever activate the *love* that is God between us and among us. And it is the experience of this love that reminds us of the deeper and truer form of belonging that we all share—our belonging to the one true and holy God who is Love.

And this brings me back around to the topic of immigration and our search for a larger moral vision of how we *belong* to one another and to God in this world. I want to end by telling three "deep stories." The first one is articulated by a journalist named Arlie Russell Hochschild after spending five years among red state Donald Trump supporters and listening to their views on economics and immigration. He tells this "deep story" as a summary of much of what is believed by these people. The second "deep story" is a parallel story that I believe captures much of what is believed by those who represent a more progressive way of thinking about economics and immigration. I then venture a derivative deep story #3 that I believe is, perhaps, the kind of story that God might want to tell the people on the Plain of Shinar, were they living today.

> The three stories approach brings key ideas and resonances into the room once we have learned their limitations, and allows for a reframing within a larger moral vision similar to what MLK Jr. would do—painting a broad stroke picture of what is hoped for within a communicative ethic.

Here, verbatim, is Hochschild's "Deep Story #1:"

You are patiently standing in the middle of a long line stretching toward the horizon, where the American Dream awaits. But as you wait, you see people cutting in line ahead of you. Many of these line-cutters are black—beneficiaries of affirmative action or welfare. Some are career-driven women pushing into jobs they never had before. Then you see immigrants, Mexicans, Somalis, the Syrian refugees yet to come. As you wait in this unmoving line, you're being asked to feel sorry for them all. You have a good heart. But who is deciding who you should feel compassion for? Then you see President Barack Hussein Obama waving the line-cutters forward. He's on their side. In fact, isn't he a line-cutter too? How did this fatherless black guy pay for Harvard? As you wait your turn, Obama is using the money in your pocket to help the line-cutters. He and his liberal backers have removed the shame from taking. The government has become an instrument for redistributing your money to the undeserving. It's not your government anymore; it's theirs.[16]

Here is Deep Story #2:

You are patiently standing in the middle of a long line stretching toward the horizon, where the American Dream awaits. But as you wait, you see people cutting in line ahead of you. Many of these line-cutters are white—beneficiaries of centuries of white privilege. As you wait in this unmoving line, you're being asked to feel sorry for white people. You have a good heart. But who is deciding who you should feel compassion for? Then you see Donald Trump waving the line-cutters forward—restricting government benefits to "real Americans only" (a dog-whistle meaning primarily "whites only"). He's on their side. In fact, isn't he a line-cutter too? How did he get into the White House except through his family's wealth and privilege? As you wait your turn, Trump is using the money in your pocket to help narrow benefits to a single insider group of mostly white line-cutters, and to line the pockets of millionaires. He and his conservative backers have removed the shame from taking federal assistance, but only if you are white and male. The government has become an instrument for redistributing your money to the undeserving. It's not your government anymore; it's theirs.

16. Hochschild, "I Spent Five Years with Some of Trump's Biggest Fans."

And here is what might be Deep Story #3

You are patiently standing in a large line in the shape of an expanding circle. At the center of the circle is God's Dream for All People. But as you wait, you see all kinds of people trying to get into the circle, people of all colors and ethnicities, all sizes and abilities, with many languages. Some are obviously suffering illness or trauma, others are jobless or under-employed. There are both educated and uneducated, urban and rural, citizen and migrant. Most of these circle-line-cutters are imperfect and human. Sometimes they are responsible, sometimes irresponsible. Sometimes they are truthful, sometimes they deceive themselves and others. Some experience themselves surviving under the weight of a long history of racism, sexism, family violence, gang violence, or political corruption. Others experience themselves as lost, hopeless, and left out, or as survivors of an economic system that has left them behind. As you wait in this circle, you're not asked to feel sorry for anyone more than anyone else, or to judge anyone. You are only asked to listen carefully to one another—to be silent and find out what is really at stake in another person's desire to join the circle—even those you like the least; even those you don't want to listen to or get to know. You have a good heart. But it is sometimes hard for you to see God waving the line-cutters forward—welcoming all kinds of people into the circle. God's not asking any of the questions you want to ask to make sure the line-cutters are worthy or meet your standards. God's just reaching out a hand to them. In fact, isn't God a line-cutter too? How did God get into the circle except through being welcomed into the hearts of those in line? As you wait your turn, you see flawed presidents and systems of government, focused more on creating straight lines than circles—but you also see that governments can sometimes be helpful when it is hard for just one or two people to welcome someone into the circle. The government, like the church, can sometimes be a practical instrument for redistributing your

> It is important in this final narrative to include "line-cutters" from both narratives in a larger vision.

money to those with the most need in situations too large or too difficult for even churches to handle. It's not your government anymore, and it's not theirs, it's ours—*all* of us.

There is some truth in the red and blue deep stories we tell ourselves. There always is. But these stories can close in on us and close us in on ourselves in our own world of insider "understanding." The God of the wilderness cannot be contained and is out there scattered among all the different people in the world. If we can be silent and listen carefully, we might be able to *hear* the voice of God in "each one of us in our own native language" (Acts 2:8). And the tower we want to build for ourselves may start to come down, the plaque can be removed, and our hearts may find a way to a new kind of belonging that can only be *listened into existence,* and can never be completely understood.

The sermon ends with a summation of the sermon's entire core message. Notice that the moral imagination here resituates "belonging" at the center of empathic listening.

When and Why to Use a Communicative Ethic

As I already mentioned in the Introduction, it is my hope that preachers will avoid a one-size-fits-all approach to ethical preaching. Each context (ecclesial, social, public, geographic), and each situation (national, legislative, congregational, local) requires us to consider what approach might be best. Different issues also suggest different approaches (gay rights, immigration, abortion, climate change, fracking).

The context best suited for a communicative ethic is one in which a church is positioned well to be engaged in public theology, especially national churches or cathedrals, state capital congregations, historic civil rights congregations, and other well-known public opinion leadership churches. Churches such as Riverside Church in New York City, Foundry Methodist Church in Washington, DC, Trinity United Church of Christ in Chicago, or Dexter Avenue Baptist Church in Montgomery, Alabama are good examples of congregations where preaching in search of broad moral consensus has had a home in different generations.

This approach also fits well in contexts where church members are well-educated and/or consider themselves to be broad-minded and forward-thinking. University congregations or churches in university or college towns often make a good contextual fit.

Communicative ethic preaching is best suited to moral issues where subject positions are strong, clearly defined, and easily identifiable. Abortion, immigration, and gun violence, for instance, have well-defined sides, along with movements and clearly stated public and policy statements and positions. Such issues lend themselves to forums, debate, rational negotiation, and consensus-seeking.

Communicative ethics is also useful in situations of national, regional, or local crisis, where discovering and proclaiming ideas that have a universal and binding/bonding aspect are crucial. We noted Jeremiah Wright's 9/11 sermon earlier. Other good examples include Martin Luther King, Jr.'s sermon on "The Crisis in the Modern Family" preached at Dexter Avenue Baptist church, in which he looked at the impact of war, urbanization, industrialization, and individualism on the American family. Or consider Horton Davies's sermon, "Christianity in the Atomic Age," preached in London at the time of the bombing of Japan. Such sermons go in search of the moral high ground in situations of public, national, or global crisis.

Most of all, a communicative ethic is required when the preacher decides that what is needed is clarity, good judgment, moderation, mediation, and pursuit of the binding/bonding moral high ground between all persons. This will include any situation where divisiveness is destroying the fabric of the civility, decency, honesty, truthfulness, and the shared hopes and dreams that motivate and inspire all persons.

Situational Sermon Example:
Communicative Ethic

Rev. Dr. James Forbes was the pastor of Riverside Church in New York City, succeeding the Rev. William Sloane Coffin. In 2007, after eighteen years of service, Forbes retired to become president of the Healing of the Nations Foundation. This sermon was preached on the second Sunday of Advent, three months following the terrorist attacks on the World Trade Center and the Pentagon. At the time, patriotic fervor and American exceptionalism ran high, and the song *God Bless America* had become a staple at professional sports events and at other large gatherings. In this sermon, Forbes seeks a more universal moral understanding of what would make America truly exceptional.

Romans 8:28

We know that all things work together for good to them that love God, to them who are the called according to God's purpose. (KJV)

Lectionary Texts for the Second Sunday in Advent
ROMANS 15:4–13
Isaiah 11:1–10
Psalm 72:1–7, 18–19
Matthew 3:1–12

Sermon preached at the National Cathedral
December 9, 2001
James Forbes

Brothers and sisters, it is always a delight for me to come to share in the worship life of this community. This is a special place aesthetically, and it also achieves a spiritual sense of place where God is present and where our lives are to be enriched as we share together in Christ's name.

You should know that I feel a special sense of comfort in being present with my friend, Dean Baxter. We have known each other for many years, and in some sense you should know that by prayer, I am implicated in his ministry here, and I have a sense that at Riverside Church in New York, we benefit from the grace that is shed in this place.

Now I want to speak out of the experience of the last few months, three months almost now since that tragic day in September when we experienced the shaking of the foundations of our national pride and sense of security and power. The Negro spiritual intones these words, "My Lord, what a morning when the stars began to fall." How very true.

My Lord, what a morning, when the World Trade Center Towers and a wall of the Pentagon began to fall. My Lord, what a morning, when symbols of our economic strength and military might were mocked, maligned, and massacred by the madness of human beings enslaved in flight and used for missiles of mass destruction.

It's autumn, into winter now, but the autumn of 2001 has witnessed more than falling leaves. Confidence, hope, trust, our economy, bombs and babies, bullets and bread and peace talks, falling around us.

But thanks be to God, we have made it through somehow! And the second Sunday of Advent is here. We've come this far by faith leaning on the Lord. Our souls look back and wonder how we got over.

Now my job this morning is to share with you something about what has been helpful to me since that awful day. And also to suggest a possible response we might make individually and as a nation to the events we continue to lament.

Here's where it started for me. From early childhood my parents used to quote from the King James Version, Romans 8:28. Whenever we children experienced bad things, sooner or later somebody would remind us, "and we know that all things work together for good to them that love God, to them who are the called according to God's purpose." This theological perspective became almost instinctual for me in reaction to any tragic situation. Now I never thought at all that God caused, or even willed, atrocities and barbarous action, but I was convinced from my youth up that nothing could happen but that God could find a way in the midst of the rubble, to bring some good out of it. This angle of understanding was later expressed, just right for me, by the late John Bennett, who was once the President of Union Theological Seminary, who said, "God does not will everything. But God wills something out of everything." That's right, I think. That's just about right.

Now, you notice that to the confidence that God is at work in everything, there is also in Romans 8:28 the requirement that we discern what we are supposed to do in the midst of the crisis. Remember the verse said, "and we know that all things work together for good to them that love God," that's God's purposes, but then, "also to those who are called according to God's purpose." It is not only that God is at work in the situation, but you and I and our brothers and sisters from far and near, we have our responsibility to find that good thing to extract from the awful circumstances, something that is positive. My faith calls me that way.

My faith calls me, yes, to hope and to action. It speaks to me like this: if tragedy strikes, make it pay dearly with something that is a greater good than the evil which has been done. My faith tells me: upstage death and destruction by amazing grace. So, go on. Tally the dead, the maimed, buildings destroyed, evil impulses fanned into dishonorable deeds, dollars lost, wars raged, liberties subverted, and ideals abandoned. Calculate, if you will, the magnitude of the horror. And then, set to work, with God, and do not rest until unnumbered blessings break out in a tidal wave of righteous deeds. Or until the earth be full of the knowledge of God as the waters cover the sea.

Since September 11th, out of my Romans 8:28 sensibilities, I have been on constant vigil, looking for that something God wills now. And that something that I, and we together, are called to do in service of God's purpose. What we have experienced—the attack, the threats, anthrax, the retaliations, and retaliatory counter-threats—these things have been so disturbing, so disorienting, and so depressing that one really has to strain one's eyes through the dust, the clouds, and continuing smoke from out of the rubble at Ground Zero, and the media glut of war reports. One has to strain to see out of all of this the greater good, and our place in God's ordained path to peace, justice, and compassion.

Well, I'm glad to report, I'm seeing some grace. I'm glad to report on what I have seen. Thanks be to God, grace has made a welcomed appearance here and there in the last few months. The heroic acts of compassion, magnanimity of spirit, blood donors, volunteers, contributors, candles honoring the dead, businesses caring for families of their lost loved ones, the almost parental attention of political leaders in New York and in Washington and around this nation, and the speed with which assistance agencies have responded, and the benefit concerts, and in general, the discovery in America of a tenacity and a resiliency of spirit, and a basic human goodness in the hearts of our fellow citizens. That's some grace working out of that disgraceful moment.

And also, I've seen some grace in the way faith communities of different religious traditions have responded in funerals, memorial services, counseling, social service ministries, and strong advocacy for tolerance and restraint befitting a truly democratic society.

And I've also seen the ground swell of expressions of patriotism, the waving of the flag, and also pausing at curtain call time at Broadway plays and sports events and even at the stock exchange, for the heart-felt singing of "God Bless America."

And I recognize that some of us sing "God, Bless America" in relatively safe space, and yet there are others who even now, in places of great peril to their lives, are doing the best they can according to their understanding to help things be better for those of us around the world who love freedom.

So I say, thanks be to God, for these fragments of grace in these never-to-be-forgotten days of doom and gloom.

But today, today, I want to report on what may prove to be the most significant blessing to emerge from the impact of 9/11.

Let me say it first interrogatively. Could it be, that out of the crisis brought by the attacks of September 11th, our nation will come to see the need for a great spiritual awakening? Can you imagine the promise of a spiritually renewed United States of America, at work with God in this time of terror, offering itself as a spiritually grounded and re-energized nation, ready to fulfill its destiny as the leader of a coalition of compassionate nations, uniting to lift up justice, peace, equality, respect, and compassion, as the foundation stones of a viable society in this age of globalization?

Well, let me acknowledge something. I have introduced this idea in the form of a question. But if I tell the truth, there is no question in my mind. I must acknowledge that really, it's more than a question. It's even more than a suggestion. Today, I stand in this pulpit with a conviction indicative of what I think God is longing to do for the good of nation, and God is longing to have us join in participation for a purpose even grander than our nationalistic longing for repair and recovery of our pride and power and our premiere place as the only super power on earth.

That's what I want to say. I want to say to everybody in the choirs and around, that out of the awful circumstances of September 11th, if we listen carefully, we may hear God saying, "Alright now, don't you see, a nation that was built upon a respect for a God who wills all of us to have life, liberty, and the pursuit of happiness. That nation cannot fulfill its destiny if it has broken sensitivity and contact with the God who has willed us to be this grand and glorious nation." And so, that's what I want to tell you.

I simply want to give you an outline of that possibility. I stand here salivating, no ventilating, out of anticipation that maybe out of all of this, just possibly, the United States of America may find its way back to a sense of spiritual grounding for the lifting up of the democratic ideals. Without God's presence and power we can't get it done now. And so that's what I wanted to talk about.

And my time's just about up already!

But let me tell you how I came to this conviction. Well, it's like this. For some time now I've been feeling that my life has no other major purpose than spiritual revitalization of the nation. And I've been talking this a long time. Way back in 1984, God said, "This is what's got to happen. We got to have spiritual revitalization wherever you go. That's what you are working on." But this 9/11, I found myself renewed in that conviction. I was so conflicted between my pastoral duties after that time, and my prophetic responsibility after that time, until I didn't even feel it was safe to go outside of my house without first of all checking in with the Spirit. I even wrote a little song that I try to sing before I go out into the streets.

"Holy Spirit, lead me, guide me, as I move throughout this day. May your guidance deep inside me, show me what to do and say. In the power of your presence, strength and courage will increase. In the wisdom of your guidance is the path that leads to peace."

So I was beginning, day by day, to say, "Holy Spirit, I don't think it's safe for me to leave my house without getting some clue from you about what I ought to do." And then one Sunday morning, this Holy Spirit thing was stirred up again in me, when they had down at Ground Zero, out of the rubble, a white pigeon came up. And I don't know what the rest of the folks thought about it but given my background with respect to doves and turtledoves and pigeons and all, when I see something white like that flying up, I just happen to think about the Holy Spirit. So there it was again!

And then as people were singing, "God Bless America," I got the impression, especially from Romans 8 in another place where it says, "the Spirit makes intercession for us according to the mind of God." And we don't know how to pray as we ought, but I heard my nation singing that song, and many of them didn't know it, but the Holy Spirit had seized that song and heaven thought America was actually praying, when they were singing, "God Bless America, land that I love. Stand beside her and guide her through the night, with the light from above." All the angels stopped and the whole heavens said, "Listen, all America is praying to us in the light of this event."

I thought about that. And then I thought I wonder what will it be like if God really thinks we were praying that our nation might be blessed? What would it look like if God actually would bless America? I got to thinking that if this is a prayer, maybe God will grant the United States of America an audience. And if God granted us an audience, maybe there would be a change. Perhaps we would get a chance to ask God, "God, tell us, why does someone hate us this much?" And God might give a much different answer than you pick up here and there. We might ask God, "God, is there anything we need to change, or to strengthen about our national purpose, that will make it better for us?" We could change that exchange with God. We could talk with God about, "God, what have we left undone on the home front? And what have we done in relationship to the Third World? And, God, is there a path that we could take that could really give us sustained peace so we can promote democracy as the leader of the free world?"

If God gives us an audience, can you imagine what that would be? In fact, I want everybody to think about this, every time you hear that song sung, "God Bless America." Think of it as God says, "OK, I'm listening, what have you got to say? And what do you have to ask? And what will it look like from your perspective if I would bless your nation?"

Of course, if you sing that song in God's presence, you might have to sing it like, . . . well, . . . even God as we say "God Bless America," we understand that the United States of America is not America. The United States is a part of a hemisphere. And then there's North America, and then there's South America, and there's Central America. And I don't think we'd want to come before God asking God to bless us to the neglect of the rest of the Americas. You see what I'm trying to say?

I'm talking about if, if we're really praying this prayer to God. We got to broaden it out. In fact, when my predecessor, Bill Coffin, said, "that when you go to God, you've got to ask for a blessing for Afghanistan too." If you're asking "God bless America," you've got to throw in some other numbers, or else God will think you are coming before the courts of glory asking for preferential treatment when God says all the children of the earth are my children. You have to be careful how you sing that song if God is listening!

And furthermore, if uncharacteristic of me, you know that I don't preach from the lectionary most of the time. But Dean

Baxter sent me all four Lessons. And I have read those Lessons over and over again, at least ten times. I mean, you read the Lessons for Advent too. They're right there in your bulletin. Read them over and over.

Let me tell you what happened to me. When I read the Isaiah passage about the righteousness of God being like water that covers the sea, and how the Root out of Jesse was going to be filled with the Spirit of wisdom and knowledge and counsel and might, the Holy Spirit got active again in me. Even though I'm being finished off in my refinement at Riverside, the Holy Ghost got active again in me because I'm hearing in this Isaiah passage that the Holy Spirit is just pulsing, just waiting for America to truly act for God-living dynamic, wisdom, justice, power and compassion. I mean, even the Psalm . . . I was going to leave the Psalter out, but it's talking about a nation, asking that our rulers will be endowed with grace, and that they will be champions for the needy, and that they will be ones who will look toward lifting the banners, the barriers of oppression from those. The Psalm had it.

And then I read the Epistle. The Epistle! I mean, let me tell you how it ended, and the Spirit is getting stirred up all the time. Notice the Epistle ended, "may the God of hope fill you with all joy and peace in believing so that you may abound in hope, by the power of the Holy Spirit." Let me tell you the Holy Spirit's getting stirred up in me.

I think God is intending to call America to spiritual revitalization. And as if that were not enough, did you all listen to the Gospel?

Additional Reading

Burghardt, Walter J. *Preaching the Just Word.*

Coffin, William Sloane. *The Collected Sermons of William Sloane Coffin: The Riverside Years.*

Forbes, James. *Whose Gospel? A Concise Guide to Progressive Protestantism.*

Gilbert, Kenyatta R. *Exodus Preaching: Crafting Sermons about Justice and Hope.*

King, Martin Luther, Jr. *A Gift of Love: Sermon from "Strength to Love" and other Preachings.*

McClure, John S. *Speaking Together and With God: Liturgy and Communicative Ethics.*

Moiso, Aimee. "Standing in the Breach: Conflict Transformation and the Practice of Preaching," *Homiletic* 45.1 (2020) 13–22.

Mumford, Debra. *Envisioning the Reign of God: Preaching for Tomorrow,* especially chapters 2, 3, 6, and 10.

Resner, André, Jr. *Just Preaching: Prophetic Voices for Economic Justice.*

Thomas, Frank. *How to Preach a Dangerous Sermon.*

———. *Surviving a Dangerous Sermon.*

Wogaman, J. Philip. *Speaking the Truth in Love: Prophetic Preaching to a Broken World.*

2

Witness Ethics

A WITNESS ETHIC STANDS in stark contrast to a communicative ethic. The optimistic commitment to the binding/bonding of society through the ongoing renegotiation of better and more universal moral norms disappears in this approach. Those who subscribe to a witness ethic believe that we have to resist this "accommodationist mode" of preaching, where sermons strive to confirm a common moral experience rather than to "challenge the presumption that we even understand what it is we assumed we have experienced."[1] Witness ethic preachers see themselves in an essentially agonistic (aggressive, competitive, political) interactive situation, saturated with tremendous, unresolvable conflict between competing narratives about right and wrong. By integrating a nonviolent and more or less sectarian view of the church from the Anabaptist wing of the Reformation with ideas from the Yale school of postliberal theology, and the virtue ethics of Alasdair MacIntyre, scholars such as Charles Campbell, William Willimon, and Stanley Hauerwas have forged different kinds of witness ethics for preaching.[2] These scholars argue that within the larger society, grossly anti-Christian ideologies and

1. Willimon and Hauerwas, *Preaching to Strangers.*

2. Campbell, *Preaching Jesus;* Willimon and Hauerwas, *Preaching to Strangers*; Lindbeck, *The Nature of Doctrine;* Frei, *The Eclipse of Biblical Narrative.*

systems hold sway, including capitalism, Constantinian Christianity, Enlightenment reason and individualism, neoliberalism, secularism, and others. Each of these metanarratives is forcefully and sometimes violently attempting to have its own way. Many of these narratives are intertwined in ways that increase both their power in the marketplace of ideas and their grip on the financial and material well-being of some at the expense of others.

An ethic of witness is not an intersubjective ethic (communicative ethics) but a *virtue* or "moral agency" ethic.[3] The preacher is involved in character-development work, helping listeners claim unique forms of Christian moral agency in the public arena. Instead of trying to pragmatically generate a new, potentially unifying moral imagination aiming at the common good, the form of action most required by the preacher in this approach is to become a *witness*, to adopt what Walter Brueggemann calls a "counteridentity" that asserts "a deep, definitional freedom from the pathologies, coercions, and seductions that govern our society."[4] Preaching is shaped in such a way as to construct a countercultural community of Christian virtue, a beacon of light on a hill celebrating and living out the gospel story.

Many theologians in the Liturgical Movement adopted this same way of thinking. These theologians were deeply concerned that the Constantinian church of Christendom was, and still is, co-opted by the dominant culture. With this in mind, these scholars returned to pre-Constantinian liturgical texts (for instance, the *Apostolic Constitutions*) in order to see what a post-Constantinian church might look like. The pre-Constantinian church was in a missionary posture up against many heretical religions and imperial forces. Scholars observed something like a witness ethic at work, in which the church created a powerful liturgical drama to set itself apart from the world around it. The Liturgical Movement, therefore, strove to restore the strangeness and drama of Christian worship: large loaves of bread on tables in plain view, larger and more available baptismal fonts, a liturgical calendar

3. For more on moral agency, see Snarr, *All You That Labor*, 5, 39.

4. Brueggemann, *Cadences of Home*, 12.

that could compete with the civic calendar, dramatic Easter Vigils that celebrated dying and rising with Christ, and a theology of radical new creation, the emergence of the "second Adam." A preacher in this liturgical drama refuses to translate or accommodate the biblical narrative to the demands of public discourse, and instead celebrates the oddness of biblical language, inviting people *into* that strange new narrative as the primary story for living ethically in society. Rather than trying to find common ground at the intersection of many competing narratives, the witness ethic preacher works to create a distinct countercultural community that orders its life around peacemaking, forgiveness, and love. This ethical approach both *critiques* and *resists* the larger society by creating an alternative community of witness through its inner communal and liturgical life.

As Sally Brown has shown, two other movements in the recent theological landscape also contribute to a witness ethic: missional theology (Darrel Guder, David Bosch), and what she calls the "faithful practices" movement (Dorothy Bass, Craig Dykstra). Missional theologians see Christians as a "sent" people, bearing distinctive gospel witness (the *missio Dei*) in a post-Christendom world. Faithful practices theologians, taking their cue from Alasdair MacIntyre's understanding of practices as human activities that render specific "internal goods," argue that the Christian witness is expressed primarily through a unique set of practices that are generative of a clearly identifiable "moral community" at work in the world.[5] In all of its forms, a witness ethic leans away from attempts to find thin universal moral norms, and toward emphasizing the unique mission of the confessing church as it lives ever more deeply into its own unique moral agency in the world.

The Way Out

For the preacher as witness ethicist, the primary problem is what Marva Dawn once called a "dumbing-down" of the Christian

5. Brown, *Sunday's Sermon for Monday's World*, 9–17. MacIntyre, *After Virtue*, 197.

faith, accommodating it to the larger culture by translating its unique language and witness into thin, publicly accessible moral norms.[6] When this occurs, Christian faith is in danger of assimilation. The uniqueness of the Christian witness is at stake. Two homiletical practices in particular are important for countering this tendency.

Exposing the Domination System

For the witness ethic preacher, the Christian is up against what the Apostle Paul called the "principalities and powers" (Rom 8:38; Col 2:15), or what Walter Wink calls the "Domination System."[7] Part of what the Domination System does is to co-opt our language, ethical sensibilities, and behavior. Under its sway we allow certain things to occur all around us that are utterly incommensurate with the gospel: capital punishment, torture, mass incarceration, white privilege, sexism, and so on. What is required is the assertion of a unique Christo-praxis that stands as an uncompromising witness *against* this Domination System. The way out, then, is, as Charles Campbell puts it, to "preach Jesus," by which he means preach Jesus as God's *nonviolent witness against this System*. Witness preachers preach the nonviolent work of Christ as an alternate grammar to the grammar of abusive power narrated by the Domination System. Sermons perform and improvise this alternative grammar without attempting to translate it or make sense out of it in the public realm. For this reason, Campbell accentuates the image of the preacher as "fool for Christ."[8] The way out of accommodation and assimilation to the Domination System is to become Christ-fools, resisting that system after the pattern of Christ who would not seize power over, or play the domination game, and who gave up that kind of life in order to save true life.

---

6. Dawn, *Reaching Out Without Dumbing Down*.

7. Wink, *Engaging the Powers*.

8. Campbell and Cilliers, *Preaching Fools*.

Using the Bible as a Script

The Bible becomes a persuasive tool in a witness ethic. It exists as "an artistic, rhetorical proposal of a reality that seeks to persuade (convert) to an alternative sense of God, world, neighbor, and self."[9] The goal of preaching is to make the Bible into an alternative script for reality—to use it to help people learn a new mother tongue that will help them re-describe and reimagine their personal, relational, ethical, and spiritual situation.[10] Sermon listeners don't have to settle for any of the dominant cultural, social, or political narratives. They have a peculiar and contrasting script (Scripture) that casts the shadow of an entirely different narrative paradigm onto history, encouraging dramatic new forms of moral agency.

The Way In

The way into confronting ethical issues within a witness ethic is through confronting one's co-optation by the Domination System and engaging in radical re-inculturation into the Christo-praxis at the heart of Scripture. Two homiletical practices can help to lead people into embracing a witness ethic: providing convincing exemplars of co-optation by the principalities and powers, and catechizing listeners into the unique language and practices of Christian faith.

Providing Convincing Examples of Co-optation

Sermon illustrations, which are always crucial for providing a way into ethical practices, will illustrate how the Domination System works by showing examples of people being subtly or not-so-subtly co-opted by this System. Often these are moments in which someone's complicity in the work of the Domination System comes into view: a bystander to bullying or abuse, a guard at an immigrant

9. Brueggemann, *Cadences*, 12.

10. Brueggemann, *Cadences*, 23–24.

detention center observing children herded into cages. Sometimes these will be stories of what Charles Campbell calls "radicalizing moments,"[11] during which someone has a realization about the powers and what they are doing to destroy their own lives or the lives of others. These examples help to convince sermon listeners of the possibility of their own complicity with the Domination System, and of the opportunity for their own self-awareness and change.

Becoming a Catechetical Teacher

In order to avoid co-optation by the dominant culture, it is important to invite sermon listeners into an alternative universe of meaning and action. Preaching becomes a central part of a larger re-inculturation process and the preacher participates in this process by assuming a catechetical role, teaching the unique language and practices of the church. In some traditions, this kind of preaching is embedded within a larger liturgical inculturation process that Robert Webber calls "liturgical evangelism."[12] This involves a one- or two-year-long catechumenate during which people are taught and trained in the dramatic, singular nature of Christian faith, participate in training exercises, and then are baptized or undergo a "renewal of baptism" at a special Easter Vigil where they "renounce evil and its power in the world."[13] The goal is to renounce one's co-optation by the Domination System and become Bible-people, or more specifically Christ-people within the larger culture, witnesses to an original and extraordinary way of life.

Whereas liberation ethic preachers see teaching from the pulpit as consciousness-raising (*conscientization*, see below), witness ethic preachers are committed to (1) teaching the unique language and concepts of the church, and (2) teaching the unique practices of the church. First, preachers enculturate listeners into the lexicon of biblical faith in all of its strangeness, teaching a new

11. Campbell, *The Word Before the Powers*, 115.

12. Webber, *Liturgical Evangelism*.

13. This language is from the Covenant of Baptism service in the Presbyterian Church (USA) *Book of Common Worship*, 407.

vocabulary to replace the language of the dominant culture. Witness ethic preachers are committed to teaching the meaning of words such as *salvation, atonement, prophecy, martyrdom, faith, mercy, apocalypse* (revelation), and *resurrection.* Second, according to Sally Brown, witness preachers help people understand the full, radical, and distinctive nature of Christian practices.[14] According to Brown, these practices fall under five categories: (1) practices of worship, (2) practices of education and formation, (3) fellowship-building and caregiving practices, (4) practices of public service and witness, and (5) practices of discernment and decision-making.[15] Preachers as catechists teach both the mother tongue of the Christian faith and the practices that are the distinctive marks of Christian faith and character.

The Way Through

Witness preachers make use of several unique ways of shaping messages as signposts for navigating any ethical landscape. Primarily, these include naming the powers, remembering past suffering, boldly taking a stand and testifying, developing ironic ways to subvert assumptions, and identifying with ordinary Christian exemplars.

Naming the Powers

First, as we have already noted, messaging will expose, and even name, the principalities and powers. Metaphors and names are chosen with care and will sometimes seem foolish or hyperbolic: monsters, machines, perpetrators, monstrosities, diabolical, invaders, enemies, calculating, hungry. Every preacher on Sunday morning must imagine that they are a street preacher standing on street corners, or a protester walking into circumstances (boardrooms, situation rooms, stockholders' meetings) where the principalities

14. Brown, *Sunday's Sermon for Monday's World,* 102–32.
15. Brown, *Sunday's Sermon for Monday's World,* 107.

and powers are most palpable and potentially dangerous. Campbell tells the story of a personal trip to Korea during which he found himself standing in a small pulpit looking out an observation window toward the demilitarized zone between North and South Korea. It is in such places that witness preachers locate themselves and their listeners in their theological imaginations on Sunday mornings, as "preaching fool(s) proclaiming a foolish gospel that fools the world."[16] It is to these contested spaces that preachers travel each Sunday morning on their way through an ethical dilemma: naming and exposing the Domination System.

Embodying Dangerous Memory

Witness preachers harbor what Johann Baptist Metz once called a "dangerous memory."[17] They remember, and will not let us forget, the past suffering in the world caused by the Domination System. The suffering of the Holocaust, the suffering of slavery, the suffering of the homeless and the unemployed, the suffering of immigrants and those without health care, all remind us of the ongoing legacy of the principalities and powers. A key signpost on the way to the realm of God includes the stories of those who are victims and survivors of the Domination System.

Testifying!

Witness ethic preaching often becomes the language of immediate testimony, a "here I stand" word of opposition and resistance. Certain things are clearly not acceptable within the Christian narrative and must be opposed and resisted at all costs. Witness preachers identify those things that must be resisted within our society, especially things that do violence to persons, communities, or the environment. Anna Carter Florence imagines this kind of testimony within the framework of the dominant culture

16. Campbell and Cilliers, *Preaching Fools,* 126.

17. Metz, *Faith in History and Society.*

that wants to silence certain voices of opposition. She calls this moment in preaching a refusal to "answer correctly or die"—a refusal to "submit to these terms," which constitutes a refusal to "give up your testimony."[18] She imagines the preacher in a "moment of reckoning" giving testimony to the truth while surrounded by voices shouting "Nonsense!"[19]

Cultivating Irony and Laughter

Witness ethic preachers may occasionally make use of dramatic, carnivalesque, or theatrical elements that turn witnessing into an intrusive or nonconforming wedge within public situations. Such acts refuse to conform to the dominant tone or tenor of a situation, and are sometimes ironic or interruptive. In this way the sermon "laughs at 'final truths,'" "challenges unchanging, established order and ideology," while "it underlines the possibility of change and renewal."[20] For instance, when in prison in South Africa during the anti-Apartheid conflict, Nelson Mandela was given the task of deciding what music would be played over the public address system for all of the prisoners. One might expect that he would choose music of great gravitas, perhaps invoking tragic historical sensibilities. His choice: Dolly Parton's music, especially *Jolene*, which was played many times at his request.[21] In another instance, during an environmental parade in New York City, students at Auburn Seminary constructed a mock-up of Noah's ark and inhabited it as a parade float. In another situation, Bishop Eugene Robinson preached a sermon at First Presbyterian Church in New York City and then led many sermon listeners out onto the parade route of a gay-rights celebration, offering cups of water to hot, thirsty participants. The carnivalesque aspect of these forms of resistance, and their nonconformity to certain assumptions, should not be missed.

18. Florence, *Preaching as Testimony*, 152.
19. Florence, *Preaching as Testimony*, 152.
20. Campbell and Cilliers, *Preaching Fools*, 134–35.
21. Abumrad, *Dolly Parton's America, Episode 6.*

Embracing Christian Exemplars

Finally, witness preachers embrace ordinary forms of resistive action, performed by Christians primarily, who are acting as Bible/Christ-people in the world. Typically, these are people who are operating in some small way beyond the Domination System. William Stringfellow calls them "tokens of the resurrection."[22] Sally Brown shows how individual, everyday actions can sometimes become "tactics" and "improvisations," through which ordinary persons intervene in difficult moral situations in ways that disrupt the assumed or dominant story line, derailing situations toward more redemptive purposes.[23] Identifying with and learning to identify paradigmatic, everyday Christ-actions become ways sermon listeners find their way through the ethical landscape around them, as Christians who want to learn how to live beyond the Domination System. In witness sermons, therefore, the good news arrives with illustrations focused on Bible/Christ-persons standing firm in their faith, often naively or foolishly, in the face of the principalities and powers. William Willimon, for instance, in a Fourth of July sermon preached for a large Baptist congregation, tells the story of a woman who attended a town hall meeting with a politician focused on health care. At one point, she stands and declares, "I'm a Baptist, so I'm not permitted simply to say am I satisfied with my health care plan. I've got to ask, 'Am I satisfied with my neighbor's health care plan?'"[24] These kinds of illustrations provide listeners with a way to see themselves as Christian moral agents. They see how they can operate as witnesses in the public sphere. Gone is the sophistication of moral translation and imagination. What is needed are more ordinary Bible/Christ-people witnessing to a confessional narrative and theology.

---

22. Stringfellow, *An Ethic for Christians*, 138, quoted in Saunders and Campbell, *The Word on the Street*, 80.

23. Brown, *Sunday's Sermon for Monday's World*, 41–70.

24. Willimon, sermon preached at the Ocean City Tabernacle, April 7, 2010.

The Way Toward

Ultimately, witness preachers do not see themselves as harbingers of a new public moral consensus or as bringers of justice, but as cultivators of moral agency. Successful preaching can only be measured by the creation of Christian moral virtue in the public arena. Preachers want to lead people out of lives controlled by metanarratives such as Christendom, Enlightenment, capitalism, and patriarchy, and into lives centered on becoming ordinary, nonviolent renderings of the character of Jesus Christ. They desire that the church become a place of resistance and a place where people can experience a foretaste of the peaceable kingdom. They want to create a community of Christ-like fools in the neighborhood. To a large extent, the actual congregation for this kind of preaching is not the people in the pews at all, but the Domination System which is being put "on notice." Both the preacher and sermon listeners are learning together how, in the ways they live, to preach to those powers. Both the liturgy and preaching become a kind of "boot camp" for a new kind of foolish foot soldier who has no weapons and who dares to take on the powers armed with nothing but God's word of love and peace.

Topical Sermon Example: Witness Ethic

Revelation 7:9–17

⁹ After this I looked, and there was a great multitude that no one could count, from every nation, from all tribes and peoples and languages, standing before the throne and before the Lamb, robed in white, with palm branches in their hands. ¹⁰ They cried out in a loud voice, saying,

"Salvation belongs to our God who is seated on the throne, and to the Lamb!"

¹¹ And all the angels stood around the throne and around the elders and the four living creatures, and they fell on their faces before the throne and worshiped God, ¹² singing,

"Amen! Blessing and glory and wisdom
and thanksgiving and honor
and power and might
be to our God forever and ever! Amen."

[13] *Then one of the elders addressed me, saying, "Who are*
these, robed in white, and where have they come from?" [14]
I said to him, "Sir, you are the one that knows." Then he
said to me, "These are they who have come out of the great
ordeal; they have washed their robes and made them white
in the blood of the Lamb.

[15] *For this reason they are before the throne of God,*
and worship him day and night within his temple,
and the one who is seated on the throne will shelter them.
[16] *They will hunger no more, and thirst no more;*
the sun will not strike them,
nor any scorching heat;
[17] *for the Lamb at the center of the throne will be their*
shepherd,
and he will guide them to springs of the water of life,
and God will wipe away every tear from their eyes."

On Being Good Citizens

John S. McClure

For John, the writer of the book of Revelation, the first-century
church was caught up in a struggle that was not merely spiritual
but political in nature: a struggle between citizenship in the Roman Empire and citizenship in the realm
of God. The language of this text resists
and denies all allegiance to the Roman
Empire, and attributes allegiance not to
a realm of legal power, control, and co-

> Notice that we begin with
> Scripture and the nature of
> its strange language.

ercion, but to a realm of self-sacrificial love, ruled by "the Lamb
who was slain." As John puts it: "Salvation belongs to our God
who is seated on the throne and to the Lamb." As Stanley

Saunders and Charles Campbell put it, "this is not church talk, but a social and political claim about the real ruler of the world."[25] Revelation is about Christian citizenship and its challenge to all other citizenships.

One's topic must be explicitly derived from the biblical text in the witness ethic.

In a recent book on the nature of citizenship amidst increasing global migration, the authors state: "citizenship is coexistent with borders . . . with the exercise of sovereign control. . . . The more we talk about security, the more we talk about citizenship. This is the predicament of citizenship. It feeds from the power of sovereignty to erect and maintain borders—borders that it cannot ultimately fully control. Citizenship cannot be thought outside of sovereignty and control."[26]

These days, as Americans, we have become obsessed with the idea of citizenship as the protection of national sovereignty and the control of borders. I can recall after 9/11, when the Bush administration and congress established the Department of Homeland Security, that many of my parents' generation who had been through World War II recoiled at the introduction of the language of a "homeland" into our national vocabulary. In its modern usage, this term is associated primarily with Nazi Germany, where it was used by the Nazis to refer to their own sense of national and racial identity. Today, the Department of Homeland Security oversees a massive network that patrols our borders, implements immigration policies, and responds to threats of terror. It is the organization, par excellence, that is concerned with policing and protecting American citizenship.

The goal here is to establish some uneasiness regarding the possibility of extreme forms of national citizenship.

On August 7, 2019, as agents of Homeland Security, Immigration and Customs Enforcement (ICE) agents arrested nearly 700 people as a part of a series of unannounced raids at worksites in Mississippi. For many children, it

Here, the nearness of this kind of citizenship is established.

25. Saunders and Campbell, *The Word on the Street*, 58.
26. Papadopoulos and Tsianos, "After Citizenship," 183.

was the first day of school, and they were left stranded with no parent to pick them up or meet them at home after school. Out of 154 affected children, many have still not returned to school out of fear that they, too, will have their hands zip tied and be hauled away in vans. Teachers, churches, and government agencies struggled for weeks to find places to take in children. When parents returned home, many wore ankle bracelets and were tracked to be sure they didn't return to work. Families are now on the verge of starvation, with no money coming in. Many families were suddenly split up, as one or both parents were detained or deported. This is a small portrait of what it will take to establish, protect, and control national citizenship and sovereignty in its most rigid form.

Recently, our young adults took a trip to the border wall that is being erected in southern Texas. They watched as huge pieces of the wall were hoisted into place. They listened as their tour guide and educator discussed which companies would be profiting by building the wall, companies ranging from a privately held Texas firm to publicly traded Israeli contractors. In the shadows of these walls, in make-shift camps erected near a detention center, our young adults engaged in Bible study with several immigrants who had experienced the detention centers, and who knew the stories of many who were now going through that ordeal. One immigrant said that it had taken her twenty-two years to become a US citizen, to "get my papers." And it took her fifteen years to see relatives that she and her mother left behind in El Salvador. As they read and studied our Revelation text it occurred to our youth that the immigrant stories they were hearing were similar to those that might have been told by the martyrs that John speaks about. They too were witnesses testifying to what, in fact, was actually occurring in the name of homeland security and citizenship in the American empire. They heard stories about

> Illustrations in the witness ethic will show Christians engaged in being good people of the Bible—discerning and living into the strange grammar of the biblical narrative.

> An exercise in dangerous memory that is part of a "radicalizing moment" for the young adult group.

sexually abused children and teenagers, life lived in desperation and constant fear, and yet also life lived in the constant hope that God would deliver and save.

When it comes to immigration, exclusion is not the main problem. Intolerance is not the main problem. Being close-minded or bigoted is not the main problem. Citizenship. That is the big problem. The sovereign coercive control and disciplining of other human bodies in order to build and maintain an empire and keep oneself and one's Caesar secure: that is the problem.

Here, the either-or countercultural logic of the witness ethic is made clear. The biblical vision of citizenship requires a decision or conversion in no uncertain terms.

Like the first-century church, we are in a situation where we, as Bible-believing Christians, must decide for either the sovereignty of the nation-state, or the sovereignty of God. As biblical Christians, that is our theological and moral crisis today. We need more Christians like our young adults, who read the Bible while listening to the testimonies of the martyrs whose lives are being destroyed by the principalities and powers of this world as they protect their own interests.

So what does it mean today to live as a citizen in the realm of God, rather than in Caesar's homeland? What does it mean to live under the sovereignty of God instead of the sovereignty of Caesar? What are the politics of citizenship in God's realm?

Well, if we are to discover those politics, we have to read the Bible and pay careful attention to how the Bible for us as Christians ultimately leads us to the politics of Jesus, who refused violence and coercion, refused Caesar's ways entirely—even to the point of martyrdom and death. It means belonging to no "imperial" city at all, but only belonging to the city of nonviolent, non-coercive, non-controlling, self-sacrificial love.

The countercultural nonviolent "way of Jesus" is central. The goal of the biblical narrative is to render this character—the character of the nonviolent Jesus, into existence—both then and now.

And what does this mean for how we see immigration? At the very least it means that instead of seeing immigration through the lens of citizenship, Christians see citizenship through the eyes of immigrants. Migrant reality is our reality. Immigrants remind us of our radical, countercultural freedom to never be fully integrated into any society as citizen; to always see citizenship as only where we "have our papers," but never as a destination; never as bound to our national or native homeland.

One of our young adults discovered something very powerful about the meaning of this text in Revelation. She noticed that "the one who was slaughtered becomes the shepherd." At the center of God's Realm is a Lamb who is now a shepherd (7:17). The ones, like Christ, who are in the most danger of being slaughtered by imperial power, are in fact the very faces and voices of the Lamb in our midst. It is they who show us where our *true* security and protection lies—with the Lamb who is now our good shepherd, tending a flock that cannot be controlled by border walls and detention centers.

> Again, it is a Bible-person—one of the young adults—who becomes the hero of the illustration. Her reading of Revelation uncovers a pivotal reversal from the logic of Empire.

As our young adults joined other groups who arrived to protest the border wall, one woman from another church held up a sign saying: "I'm not exactly from here either!" And that, I believe, pretty well sums it up. You and I are not exactly from here, no matter what our papers say. As Christians engaged in the politics of Jesus, we cannot protect ourselves through violence and coercion, through caging people, through "extreme vetting," putting ankle monitors on people, or sending families home to die at the hands of gangs and drug lords. We follow the slaughtered Lamb, who is now and will always be our shepherd, in whom we find our security and our hope that every tear will one day be wiped away.

> Both of these final illustrations show us everyday *Christians* who are like beacons on a hill, *witnesses* who in word and deed proclaim the strange grammar of biblical faith resisting the principalities and powers in this world.

At an immigrant rights rally on August 8, 2019, the day after the ICE raids in Mississippi, Christians from around the region gathered and proclaimed allegiance to citizenship in God's realm by condemning the practices implemented by ICE and also condemning the criminalization of migrant populations as entirely against the biblical witness. They also immediately began the process of finding ways to counsel and support children and families, provide financial relief for paying utilities and getting food, and getting legal support in place where necessary. By mid-November, the Morton United Methodist Church had collected over $100,000 to pay bills for people affected by the raid, and a Presbyterian church was collecting Christmas presents for the children.

This is a small picture of what it means to be not exactly from here either, as Christians. This is our work. This is our biblical witness—until our citizenship in God's realm is complete and the Lamb is victorious.

When and Why to Use a Witness Ethic

A witness ethic is an either/or ethic. For this reason, it is best used in situations where the preacher is completely convinced that a Christian alternative can challenge and correct all existing narratives regarding a specific ethical issue. The preacher must also be convinced that this Christian countercultural alternative is non-negotiable and is unique to the Christian narrative and its nonviolent core. This unique Christian narrative does not pander to the usual rhythms of the conservative-liberal divide. At times it may seem to lean toward more conservative approaches to an issue (sometimes this is true for abortion, for instance), and at other times it seems to lean more toward a liberal approach (on issues such as capital punishment, gun violence, or war).

A witness ethic is a "take it to the streets" ethic, and is useful in situations where active protest, civil disobedience, community organizing, or dramatic symbolic tactics are required. When Bree Newsome climbed the flagpole and removed the Confederate flag at the South Carolina statehouse while reciting, "I come against you in the name of God," she embodied a witness ethic. Such actions are in themselves sermons through which Christian moral agency is cultivated and given voice in the public square.

This ethic is often put into play in congregations or social movements that see themselves as civilly disobedient or counter-cultural sanctuary churches, safe houses, asylums, or refuges for persecuted individuals or groups of people: immigrants, refugees, GLBTQIA individuals, and others. This metaphor for the church, however, may extend to nearly every aspect of organizational life and mission. Persons in these enclaves go out into the streets and witness to something radically different and then return to celebrate that difference liturgically and homiletically.

This ethic usually requires a context where the Bible is taken seriously as the narrative that defines and motivates the alternative life of moral agency within the new nonviolent community. Because witness-ethic persons are Bible-people, there needs to be a clear focus in such communities on studying the Bible. In this study, the Bible is read through the christological lens of the nonviolent character and paradigmatic witness of Jesus of Nazareth. This ethic functions best where a Christocentric rendering of the Bible is possible, and where the Bible itself is taken seriously as the community's "Word Before the Powers."[27]

This ethic also functions best in a context where people are responsive to its catechetical and enculturating aspects. It requires an eagerness to learn a new grammar of faith (and life), and to live deeply and completely into the rituals and practices of Christian faith. This includes a willingness to enact that faith unapologetically, and sometimes "foolishly" and dramatically, in the public arena.

Finally, this ethic is helpful in contexts where it is clear that the church has been co-opted by the Domination System and the biblical witness has lost its countercultural power and been reduced to a set of moral platitudes or empty rituals. William Willimon, for instance, adopted this approach when he was the chaplain at Duke University, using it to upend what he perceived to be the triumph of Enlightenment reason, political correctness,

27. See Campbell, *The Word Before the Powers.*

and bland moralistic Christianity. Realizing that he was also operating in the deep South, where biblicism was rampant, and many students were reacting to such "unenlightened," inerrantist views, Willimon played the biblical fool for Christ, pitting a new form of anti-Enlightenment, nonviolent biblicism against the grain of the students' academic and regional culture.

In all instances, the decision for a witness ethic requires a creative desire to accentuate the uniqueness of the Christian faith and Christian moral agency in the midst of the larger culture, and an unwillingness to dumb down this uniqueness within one's congregation or community. Certain nonnegotiables require Christians to act, speak, and resist the powers that, if left unchecked, will only bring destruction—especially to those who have the least voice in our midst.

Situational Sermon Example: Witness Ethic

William Willimon was dean of the chapel at Duke University from 1984 to 2004, before becoming Bishop of the North Alabama Conference of the United Methodist Church. The sermon below was preached during the difficult years of ending apartheid in South Africa and the shift from communism to social democracy in the Soviet Union under Gorbachev. This Advent sermon demonstrates well how a witness ethic is designed to put forth the foolish "more" of the gospel narrative in a prosaic, unexpecting, and anesthetized world gripped by closed economic and political systems, reductionism, greed, individualism, self-help, and a trenchant inability to expect anything beyond the given. The narrative and poetic dimensions of a witness ethic come through strongly in this sermon.

Isaiah 61: 1, 2, 4, 11

> [1] *The spirit of the LORD GOD is upon me, because the LORD has anointed me . . . to bring good news to the oppressed, to bind up the brokenhearted, to proclaim liberty to the captives, and release to the prisoners;*
> [2] *to proclaim the year of the LORD's favor . . .*

⁴ *They shall build up the ancient ruins, they shall raise up the former devastations. . . .*
¹¹ *. . . the* L<small>ORD</small> GOD *will cause righteousness and praise to spring up before all the nations.*

More

William H. Willimon

There is more to life than meets the eye. There is more to our past than history can tell. There is more going on in the present moment than we know. There is more to our relationships with one another than we are aware of, and the more we explore the mystery of ourselves, the more mysterious our selves become. Seldom have we been content with what appeared on the surface; we know there is more. Seldom have we felt fully at ease in the present moment, sensing, however inchoately, that no matter how full our present, beyond the now there is more.

We tend, if left to our own devices, toward reductionism. Here in academia we ought to be exploring possibilities, enriching our sense of what is not known, cultivating wonder. Alas, if left to our own devices, we reduce the cosmos to the periodic table. We explain human history by reducing it to the six causes of the Civil War, the main reason for the Great Depression, thirty true/false statements explaining the eighteenth century. In our better moments, when the modern analytic gives way to the eternal poetic, we know there is more.

When life is reduced to technique, six easy steps toward sure success, flattened to a series of problems to be solved, we become numbed, anesthetized against either real pain or true pleasure. The body adjusts, in the absence of expectation, to its cage. But occasionally someone manages to hit a nerve and we, twitching slightly in discomfort, suspect that there may be more.

The audience for this Advent text from Isaiah are the afflicted, the brokenhearted, the captives, those in prison, and mourners. In short, your average Durham December congregation. The people to whom these words are addressed are those who come to church out of a sometimes barely felt, sometimes fervently burning hope for more. The words also speak (though we know not how they will hear them) to those who have stopped coming to church because they have given up hoping for anything more.

Here is what Isaiah says: God has intervened, God has anointed One to take action. That action is political—release of prisoners, reparation for the ruined cities, justice. The intervention is announced by the poetical. It's just poetry here. Poetry with dangerous (dangerous for the establishment, that is) political repercussions. The "year of the Lord" which Isaiah announces is Jubilee time, when everything to which the established political order would have us adjust is turned upside down, set right, and the devastated, empty streets of downtown Durham are transformed into a great festival.

When we were slaves in Egypt, God intervened, and we remember. We had learned to be content with our lot in Egypt. (At least in slavery our masters gave us three square meals a day.) But God intervened and led us out toward more. Intervention is needed again, some decisive intrusion that will enable new life and halt our march toward death. Israel and the church struggle to describe this intervention. Exodus. Bethlehem. Calvary. The upper room. The empty tomb. Without intervention, there is no hope, for there is no "more." And, thank God, because there is God, in circumstances of the worst brokenheartedness, captivity, imprisonment, and mourning, there is always more.

Isaiah speaks of a world beyond present arrangements, a world where there is good news, liberty, comfort, garlands, instead of ashes. This is biblical apocalyptic, Bible talk about the more beyond the now. It is daring, poetic, political speech, speech pushed to the boundaries in description of what God is breaking open among us, breaking open in dusty little out-of-the-way places like Bethlehem or Soweto. Isaiah's words refused to abide within the confines of the rationality of the dominant society, refuse to be limited by common sense. NAS's "Canon of western literature." Apocalyptic speech breaks open.

It was Isaiah who taught Mary to sing apocalyptically, "My soul magnifies the Lord, / . . . my spirit rejoices in God my savior, . . . / he has scattered the proud, . . . / he has put down the mighty from their thrones, / and exalted those of low degree; / he has filled the hungry with good things, /and the rich he has sent empty away" (Luke 1:46b–53).

When we come to church and are exposed to such speech from Isaiah or Mary, we are beckoned out beyond the world of predictability into another world of risk and gift, in which divine intervention enables new life to break our prosaic reductions, to subvert tamed expectations, to evoke fresh faith. Dangerous hope leads to daring resistance. Docility is no longer possible for those who heard tell of more.

Being interviewed on television, a group of Soviet Christian dissidents was asked by a reporter, "Well, what do you want? Why aren't Soviet Christians satisfied with the new freedoms that Gorbachev has given? Why won't you now soften your criticism and support the government?"

A Christian dissident responded, the translator explained, "He says they are not satisfied. He says they want more."

Anything less is trap and delusion. Sunday, at its best, is a summons toward more. But not just any old more. Our vague, frequently reoccurring, gnawing sense of need, which we so often attempt to assuage by more mere buying, accumulating, getting, and giving—particularly at this time of year—is articulated and reformed by the prophet as a groping after God and God's will. The "more" we desire is given a name, named "the year of the Lord's favor." The year in which God gets what God wants, when earth more closely resembles that which God first had in mind when God began forming nothing into something, less into more.

Poetic, apocalyptic, prophetic speech as that of Isaiah, or Mary, or an Advent hymn, doesn't just describe the world, it re-creates, makes a world. It is a world made open, with old, comfortable certitudes broken by the advent of a God who makes all things new. In the world where God comes, we are allowed to roam. Here is poetic imagination assaulting ideology. New configurations of life yet unformed, unthought, undreamed, now available.

"The Spirit of the Lord God is upon me, . . . good tidings to the afflicted; . . . the opening of the prison to those who are bound; . . . to give them a garland instead of ashes."

Here is Isaiah's poetic protest against religion reduced to slogan, morals, five fundamentals, bumper-sticker proverbs, thoughts for the day, religion relegated to the conventional, the boring rehash of the obvious and the already known. Here is protest against Sunday as adjustment to what is seen rather than probing of the more. We came to church for certitude, to touch base with the known, but apocalyptic speech goes beyond certitude. In the poetic, apocalyptic, Spirit-anointed space, possibility overwhelms necessity and we can breathe.

So we go forth after church. There are the same quarrels in the car on the way home, the same tensions over the dinner table, the same blue Monday. Now, however, we are aware of a new world, new hope, new possibility, new dreams, new hunger for something else—in short, we are aware of more. We see how greatly reduced, how tamed has been our truth. We, who have tasted new wine, now thirst for more.

The Prince of Darkness whispers, "adjust, adapt." The Prince wants to keep the world closed, for a closed world is easier to administer, and people without a future are more manageable than those with imagination.

Some Sundays when we gather, the Prince rules the roost. No new thing is uttered or heard. The pulpit is the place of platitudes, comfortable clichés, proverbs, slogans, and nothing more.

But sometimes, on a cold Sunday in December, we peek over the horizon, stand on tiptoes with Isaiah, and there is more. Somebody goes home from church newly discontent with present arrangements, hungry. Someone gets ready for more than just another Christmas. Advent becomes adventure. And we dare to wish for ourselves more, more for our world, more for others, and Isaiah laughs and Mary sings. Poetry has carried the day against prose, and the Prince knows that he has lost a little of his territory to its true Lord. The Lord's newly reclaimed territory is you.

"The kingdom of the world has become the kingdom of our Lord and of his Christ, and he shall reign for ever and ever" (Rev 11:15).

Did you read in the paper about the man in a depressed region of Appalachia, a coal miner out of work for months, who caught his children on the back porch thumbing through a Sears catalog, wishing. He flew into a rage, switched their legs, tore the catalog to bits, and sat down in his yard and wept. He loved them so much, he couldn't bear to see them wish for more.

Did you read in the Bible about the young woman in a depressed region of Judea, a poor unmarried mother-to-be who was caught singing for more? "My soul magnifies the Lord, . . . for he who is mighty has done great things. . . . He has scattered the proud . . . , he has put down the mighty . . . , and exalted those of low degree; he has filled the hungry with good things."

Additional Reading

Brown, Sally. *Sunday's Sermon for Monday's World: Preaching to Shape Daring Witness.*

Campbell, Charles L. *Preaching Jesus: New Directions for Homiletics in Hans Frei's Postliberal Theology.*

———. *The Word Before the Powers: An Ethic of Preaching.*

Campbell, Charles L., and Johann H. Cilliers. *Preaching Fools: The Gospel as a Rhetoric of Folly.*

Florence, Anna Carter. *Preaching as Testimony.*

Lindbeck, George. *The Nature of Doctrine: Religion and Theology in a Postliberal Age.*

Saunders, Stanley P., and Charles L. Campbell. *The Word on the Street: Performing the Scriptures in the Urban Context.*

Travis, Sarah. *Metamorphosis: Preaching After Christendom.*

Webber, Robert. *Liturgical Evangelism.*

Willimon, William H. *The Intrusive Word: Preaching to the Unbaptized.*

Willimon, William H., and Stanley Hauerwas. *Preaching to Strangers.*

3

Liberation Ethics

THE PREACHER AS LIBERATION ethicist is motivated by an unsettling awareness of systemic inequities of power and resources for selfhood that exist in the world. Some people seem to hold all of the cards. Others are left out of the game entirely. This awareness is sometimes frightful, traumatic, or painful, as the preacher or someone close to the preacher experiences their own invisibility, powerlessness, or what theologian Simone Weil calls "decreation."[1] The struggle to become a living human subject on this planet may seem overwhelming. For some preachers, it could be that some life experience or teachable moment has interrupted their self-consciousness and forced them out of a comfortable parochial world into a larger awareness of their own privileged situation, a situation that now seems to be purchased at the expense of others. This can begin a progressive and convicting awareness of the pain and suffering of the poor, the shamed, the shunned, the outcast, the abused, or the disenfranchised.

Liberation ethicists notice in the biblical testimony how God identifies over and over again with the poor, the outcast, and the stranger. God seems to take sides within the biblical narrative,

1. Weil, *Gravity and Grace*, 32. Decreation is "to make something created pass into the uncreated."

aligning God's purposes with the achievement of justice for those who have the least. In the prophetic literature, it seems that these purposes are focused not simply on performing acts of charity or reforming the existing social order, but on creating something revolutionary on the already traumatized ground of the here and now. Anticipation of that future and exploring bold new possibilities motivate the liberation ethic preacher.

Whereas a communicative ethic is an intersubjective ethic, and a witness ethic is a virtue ethic, a liberationist ethic is a *social* ethic. It aims primarily at the unmasking, critique, and change of current social systems (economic, political, religious, educational, health care, etc.). Like the witness ethic preacher, the liberation ethic preacher is an educator. Instead of catechetical education, however, the liberation preacher engages in critical education or consciousness-raising (*conscientization*) regarding the ways that social systems oppress and dehumanize. This work is not limited to persons of Christian faith, but can be expansive in nature. The liberationist is willing and eager to join ranks with any organization or religious group whose primary aim is the liberation of the oppressed. Often, consciousness-raising takes place with those who are oppressed. In this work, the formation of certain Christian virtues may occur, but it is a by-product of the work of re-education and organizing for justice.

Unlike the communicative ethicist, the liberation ethicist does not seek out theologically resonant universals to preach but emphasizes the concrete and the historical. Messages are bound to the particular struggles of certain disenfranchised groups of people within history whose lives are often invisible or disregarded. The particular struggles of these groups intersect in many ways. For this reason, liberationist ethics is sometimes identified as "intersectional" in nature, rather than universalist.[2] Liberation ethic preachers are attuned to places where the particular suffering of one marginalized group puts them in solidarity with another group.

Liberation is not simply aimed at the poor and disenfranchised. Liberation theologians point out that middle-class and

2. See Kim and Shaw, *Intersectional Theology*.

upper-class persons are also oppressed within the same systems of class, race, gender, education, health, housing, and economics. Speaking of the gentrification of San Francisco that has taken place in the past twenty years, pushing the poor into tent ghettos and homelessness, poet Tongo Eisen-Martin calls attention to the aesthetic design and feeling of the new row houses and condominiums that all look the same, and the new policing system, as a form of "strange and permanent occupation" and a "dystopia" where "even the wealthy seem to be incarcerated."[3] It is important, therefore, for the middle and upper classes to realize that they too are not free, but are oppressed by social systems that lull them to sleep with a sense of individual privilege and the power to purchase commodities.

Eunjoo Mary Kim reminds us also that in an age of globalization, oppressive systems and structures are globally interconnected. She accentuates "glocalization"—the many ways that postmodern technologies and web-based networks link local systems closely to global systems. We are now more aware than ever of how food production, air pollution, public health decisions, and market forces have an impact on the lives of everyone across all cultures and contexts. Kim argues that liberation in a global situation requires a form of humanization that reaches across cultures and contexts and becomes "transcontextual" in nature.[4] Forms of liberating praxis carried out locally can have a global impact.

The Way Out

For the preacher as liberation ethicist, the fundamental ethical problem, no matter what the issue under consideration, is what sociologist and philosopher Antonio Gramsci called "hegemony."[5] Essentially, hegemony exists as that which is taken for granted as the dominant ideology, or simply "goes without

3. Eisen-Martin, "Tongo Eisen-Martin's Brief but Spectacular Take on Poetry as Revolution."

4. Kim, *Preaching in an Age of Globalization*, 47.

5. Gramsci, *Selections from the Prison Notebooks*.

saying" for most people most of the time. In their book *The Liberating Pulpit*, Justo González and Catherine González call this "subconscious oppression."[6] Hegemony takes many forms, depending on one's point of view. For the feminist, hegemony that "goes without saying" is patriarchy. For persons of color, the obvious hegemony is white privilege. For the chronically poor, hegemony wears the face of classism and exploitation. For the colonized, hegemony looks like colonial exploitation. For the person with disabilities, that which goes without saying is cultural and social ableism—assumptions that bar entrance and engender physical exclusion. For the youth and elderly, hegemony is embodied in the ageism that undermines voice, freedom, and dignity. For GLBTQIA persons, heterosexism is the tacit code that bars access to personhood and social equality. And the list goes on. Several homiletical emphases are crucial for providing a way out of these various forms of hegemony.

Raising Consciousness

The way out of these of situations of oppression by hegemonic forces usually involves gaining crucial forms of self-knowledge through the analysis of how, in fact, various hegemonies operate. This requires some engagement with critical theories (critical race theory, feminist theory, postcolonial theory, queer theory, and others) that can help the preacher understand better how these "isms" are socially constructed and stand at the root of much of the violence and suffering in the world.

The way out can also include engaging in non-touristic cross-cultural learning that takes persons of privilege into homeless shelters, women's shelters, prisons, border crossings, or situations of poverty and mass oppression. These experiences can unsettle stereotypes and provoke awareness of the life situations of those who live beyond the seemingly safe enclosure of hegemonic privilege. Such cross-cultural learning is focused less on cultivating Christian

---

6. González and González, *The Liberating Pulpit*, 15.

moral agency (*catechesis*) and more on getting to know oppressed persons, helping them physically and materially, and working together to raise awareness of their situation. These consciousness-raising efforts help preachers identify with the poor and oppressed and informs how they describe and critique the ways that injustice inhabits and shapes their lives.

Trying New Homiletical Forms

Homiletical forms themselves have a hegemonic aspect. Considering its Greco-Roman oratorical underpinnings, the pulpit is a Western, male, and privileged construct in its current form. As Roxanne Mountford asserts, the pulpit is a "gendered space,"[7] and as others are now demonstrating, it is also shaped by classism, racism, colonialism, ageism, and ableism. Part of the way out, therefore, can mean exploring new forms of preaching that can disassociate the pulpit from practices of oppression. Lisa L. Thompson, for instance, explores some of the unique ways Black women inhabit with subversive ingenuity an historically male and masculinized Black pulpit.[8] In a similar fashion, Jennifer Copeland analyzes how women can use multiple variables within different preaching situations to shift the "feminine register" at work within the communication process.[9] Donyelle McCray explores how artistic practices such as quilting have historically been homiletical practices for women not allowed into pulpits.[10] It is also possible to consider forms of Bible-interpretive symbolic action or theatre as homiletical in nature. For instance, when Bree Newsome climbed the flagpole at the South Carolina state capitol reciting Scripture and took down the confederate flag, she was not only a symbolic fool for Christ, embodying a witness ethic, she was enacting a new non-pulpit form of preaching, embodying a liberation ethic. In

7. Mountford, *The Gendered Pulpit.*

8. Thompson, *Ingenuity.*

9. Copeland, *Feminine Registers.*

10. McCray, "Quilting the Sermon," 46.

this way, a significant part of moving beyond all forms of hegemony may involve moving beyond Euro-American forms of embodiment and preaching practice.

Being Suspicious of Usual Biblical Interpretations

Another significant aspect of the way out of hegemony is the incorporation of a hermeneutic of suspicion in the way that preachers interpret the Bible. Liberation ethic preachers suspect that what goes without saying has had an impact on most biblical commentaries. Because of this, they go in search of commentaries that start with the experience of the oppressed and marginalized, and with the sociological and political context in which biblical materials were written. Liberationist readings ask such questions of biblical narratives and texts as:

- Who is missing?
- Who goes unnamed?
- What is the social and political context?
- How are women, the elderly, the young, the poor, the ill, the disabled, the migrants, and other nations or cultures depicted in the text and why?
- How is patriarchy overlaid on this story or idea?
- What vested interest in power or privilege are present in this text?

The liberation ethic preacher's bookshelves will include commentaries written from many perspectives informed by critical theories: feminist, postcolonialist, queer, and others. They will also include commentaries that explore elements within biblical interpretations that are actually or potentially anti-Jewish, ableist, or racist. Such uncritical interpretations are usually driven, either intentionally or naively, by the commentator's position of privilege or power. Liberation ethic preachers grant priority to readings that come from the perspective of those who are frequently rendered in sermons as voiceless, or who have been stereotyped in ways that privilege those in power.

Making the Exodus Narrative and the Prophets Central

Whereas the narrative of the nonviolent Jesus is central for the witness ethic preacher, the exodus narrative holds pride of place for most liberation ethicists. This narrative expresses most of the key elements for finding a way out of oppression: awareness of sin as the social and political abuse of power, liberation of the enslaved by a God who takes sides with the oppressed, and a resulting self-reflective sense of community and commitment to God's future of justice and peace. The historical power of this narrative, especially among African American churches, has ensconced it as the central narrative marking the way out of racial hegemony within Black liberation ethics.

Biblical prophecy also claims a central role in articulating a way out of the current oppressive situation through an emphasis on God as a powerful force for a new future. For the liberation ethicist, God is not an ahistorical being, but is active eschatologically within history, revealing in present-day acts of justice the final telos of history as a realm of righteousness and peace. Because of this, liberation ethic preachers are keenly attracted to biblical prophecy and the announcement of God's future reign of peace on the earth. There can be no such peace without the prior establishment of justice. The Hebrew prophets, who show so clearly the future that God promises, hold a special theological place in the preaching of liberation ethicists.

The Way In

Liberation ethic preachers often ask, "Won't the way into an ethical issue differ if my congregation consists mostly of people who benefit from the privileges of hegemony or if it is composed of those who are mostly oppressed by hegemony?" There will be some differences. But even within congregations of the wealthy and privileged, many are, or have been, in situations where their resources for selfhood are taken away. This might include experiences of domestic abuse, unemployment, violence or military trauma, racism, or ageism. As already noted, liberation ethicists are quick to point out that the liberation of the poor is also the liberation of the wealthy, whose blindness to the world they are creating and enjoying limits their ability to know God and to experience fullness of life. With this in mind, Christine Smith offers two helpful ways for liberation ethic preachers to lead sermon listeners into an ethical issue, whether one is preaching primarily to oppressed or oppressor: *weeping* and *confession*.[11]

Weeping

By *weeping*, Smith implies that the first way into an issue is through joining in lamentation with and for those who are being oppressed or victimized. Preachers can help congregations lament the impact of unjust social systems. This might involve hearing stories or testimonies of victims or survivors, or observing clips from documentaries by journalists who have gone deep into situations of poverty or cultural marginalization. It might involve hearing the stories of those in unique yet intersecting situations of oppression in order to create, broaden, or deepen a sense of intersectional solidarity with the suffering of others. For the privileged, hearing these stories or testimonies can help to accomplish what Dawn Rae Davis calls "un-mirroring," or "a breakdown of the mirror," as the mirror of hegemony begins to crack, and the clarity of the privileged image becomes distorted and tarnished.[12] Although this way into an ethical issue must be handled carefully to avoid certain triggers, and is perhaps best used in special circumstances, testimonies of lament can be forceful ways into an issue within a liberation ethic.

11. Smith, *Preaching as Weeping, Confession, and Resistance.*
12. Davis, "Unmirroring Pedagogies."

It is also important to provide pictures of the ways oppressive social systems cast aside certain groups of people while privileging others. When preaching about immigration, for instance, a preacher might narrate stories about the lack of adequate treatment for immigrants suffering from COVID-19. In this way, preachers involve listeners in lamenting the ways that social systems often marginalize certain groups of people.

Confessing

By *confession*, Smith means a commitment to truth-telling. In many ways, confession picks up where lamentation leaves off. For the privileged, as the mirror of privilege cracks it is time to begin to tell the truth about one's active complicity in the oppression of others. In a sermon on immigration, for instance, the preacher might include testimony by detention center guards who wept as they saw families separated, and who began to confess openly, and at some personal risk, that the detention system is inhumane. For victims and survivors, what might be confessed is avoidance, hiding, or absorption in one's distress, permitting certain hegemonic forces to remain unchallenged. A sermon on immigration might include the testimony of an immigrant who finds a way to participate in a movement or organization involved in advocating for change. Whether highlighting sins of omission or commission, confession involves telling the truth about who we really are in the midst of ongoing oppression and beginning to take a stand for justice.

Stories of confession are sometimes stories of actual *conversion*. Hilary Clinton, for instance, confessed that after writing many letters to parents of dead soldiers during the Iraq war, she changed her mind regarding her previous support of that armed conflict. Her weeping with the parents had an impact and drew forth a public confession of how wrong she had been, and a conversion to a different position. In a similar way, a veteran ICE agent, convinced that new agency rules placed children "directly in harm's way," broke silence to a journalist in a 2017 *New Yorker* article about his disillusionment and change of heart.[13] These kinds of stories can offer a significant way in by seeing ourselves and people in moral situations similar to ours—looking again in the mirror and discovering what it means to change and become liberation-people in the public square.

The Way Through

For the liberation ethic preacher, several signposts are important for lighting the way through any ethical terrain. These include: showing listeners public exemplars of resistance to current social systems, emphasizing the contextual and historical nature of biblical interpretation, rethinking dominant theologies, and closely correlating the pastoral and the prophetic.

Providing Signs of Resistance

Here we come to a third element of Smith's liberation preaching: *resistance*. Smith encourages preachers to emphasize the specific oppressive reality of the social situation while providing exemplars that demonstrate what we can practically do now to resist its impact. In a sermon on immigration, for instance, resistance might take the form of a story about a whistleblower informing the media about conditions in an immigrant detention center, or protesters rallying at a section of the border wall. Liberation ethic preachers will always incorporate illustrations of people making resistive steps to challenge the status quo.

Gospel illustrations for liberation ethic preachers can also show forms of Christo-praxis where we see people altering the rules of the current system. In an immigration sermon, for instance, we might see pictures of persons actively subverting existing systems from the inside—breaking the rules about how detention centers are operated, altering the way ICE agents carry out arrests, and so on. These illustrations or stories can show us

13. Blitzer, "A Veteran ICE Agent, Disillusioned."

resistance-people creating new forms of action while still operating on the traumatized ground of a not-yet-liberated world. Unlike the witness ethic, however, where examples of Christo-praxis are primarily "Bible-people" living out their unique Christian moral agency, for the liberation ethic preacher, illustrations of the good news can be found among non-Christians as well. "Anonymous Christians" exist wherever there is conversion to the work of justice and resistance to injustice.[14]

Showing How the Bible is Contextual

Liberation ethic preachers emphasize that the Bible is *contextual* in two complementary ways. Initially, it must be read in such a way that its political and sociological contexts are foregrounded. Messages to, from, or about the poor, women, the disabled, the elderly, immigrants, and many who are barely named or go unnamed are sought out, and the political and social dimensions of the text become crucial to its interpretation. The second contextual aspect involved in reading the Bible is more current in nature. Congregations are made aware of how ethical questions and issues arising in our context today draw forth trajectories of meaning from the biblical text that could not have been seen before our current situation. The civil rights movement, for instance, helped preachers see previously hidden trajectories of meaning in the biblical text. The same is true for the feminist movement. In short, liberation preachers always help listeners see that the Bible has a context and it speaks into a context.

Reframing Theology

The liberation ethic preaching applies a hermeneutic of suspicion to all commonly accepted theologies. An important set of messages help sermon listeners understand how aspects of many traditional theologies can perpetuate oppression. What does it mean,

14. Hare, *Interpretation: Matthew*, 291.

for instance, to say that pride is sin among those who do not have enough of a sense of self to have pride? What happens if we tell abused spouses to "forgive seventy times seven" (Matt 18:22)? What is the relationship between forgiveness and justice? What differences or distinctions should be made between survival and liberation as aspects of a liberation theology? What distinctions should be drawn between types of suffering ("natural" vs. inflicted, chosen vs. systemically imposed, voluntary vs. involuntary, etc.)? The way through ethical issues for the liberation ethic preacher will always involve theological reframing and reinterpretation.

Showing How the Prophetic
is Pastoral (and vice versa)

Liberation ethic preachers often yoke together pastoral and prophetic messages. This is because pastoral care is also understood contextually and systemically. Personal trauma and social trauma are closely knit. The unannounced raid and arrest of hundreds of immigrant workers at a meat processing plant in Mississippi left dozens of children stranded at schools or at bus stops with no one to pick them up and take them home. In that instance, the social trauma of labor deportation inflicted personal trauma on children and families. The same connection between the personal and the political is true for personal acts of resisting oppressive systems. For instance, a bus driver in California chose to stop two blocks before an ICE roadblock to let immigrants off the bus. His personal act of care for his daily bus riders, and the political situation of heavily enforced deportation, were of one piece.

The Way Toward

Liberation theology is, above all else, a theology of hope. It is a toward-theology. Liberation hope, however, is not utopian. It is measured and material in nature. It looks for the survival and flourishing of all living things in their material and embodied forms.

Socially, as Eunjoo Mary Kim emphasizes, liberation means a radical form of *humanization*: personal, interpersonal, intersubjective, and social.[15] This involves the humanizing of economic relations, education, social structures, and political systems. As dehumanizing aspects are resisted and jettisoned, the possibility for the survival and flourishing of human life in all of its myriad forms comes into view. Humanization means that all persons, and all cultures, are provided the same resources for selfhood and subjectivity. Everyone is able to claim their own God-given creative powers for being and becoming as human beings. This humanized social world is the liberation ethic preacher's hope, and it is what each sermon aims at and seeks to move listeners toward.

Liberation ethicists are realistic and forward-thinking. They are not nostalgic. They do not believe one can retreat historically or existentially behind racism, colonialism, sexism, classism, or ageism. Liberation hope, therefore, never allows otherworldly images of "streets paved with gold" to interfere with a clear-headed awareness of current injustices. Hope is built on the burnt ground upon which we stand, and involves struggle, imagination, and bold experimentation.

Although this kind of hope can seem minimal, only to be perceived in what Miguel De la Torre calls the "shards of life,"[16] it is traceable wherever human misery and exploitation is eliminated, and unjust social structures are uprooted and replaced. As James Cone points out, we also see it whenever we see repentance, conversion, and participation in communities and movements that are involved in liberating work.[17] This participation includes the awakening of both the oppressed and the oppressor (conscientization) and the organization of popular movements within various sectors of public life in order to bring about public and political change. When we see such activity, we see the reign of God at work. Unlike proponents of the social gospel, for liberation ethicists the arrival of the reign of God is not an evolutionary certainty. All

15. Kim, *Preaching in an Age of Globalization*, 43–64.
16. De la Torre, *The Politics of Jesús*, 139.
17. Cone, *A Black Theology of Liberation*, 125–26.

of these shards have a provisional quality, subject to what Johann Baptist Metz called the "eschatological proviso," through which the future ultimately belongs to God, not simply to Christians inspired by the suffering Christ in the world.[18]

Topical Sermon Example: Liberation Ethic

Matthew 25:31–46

[31] *"When the Son of Man comes in his glory, and all the angels with him, then he will sit on the throne of his glory.* [32] *All the nations will be gathered before him, and he will separate people one from another as a shepherd separates the sheep from the goats,* [33] *and he will put the sheep at his right hand and the goats at the left.* [34] *Then the king will say to those at his right hand, 'Come, you that are blessed by my Father, inherit the kingdom prepared for you from the foundation of the world;* [35] *for I was hungry and you gave me food, I was thirsty and you gave me something to drink, I was a stranger and you welcomed me,* [36] *I was naked and you gave me clothing, I was sick and you took care of me, I was in prison and you visited me.'* [37] *Then the righteous will answer him, 'Lord, when was it that we saw you hungry and gave you food, or thirsty and gave you something to drink?* [38] *And when was it that we saw you a stranger and welcomed you, or naked and gave you clothing?* [39] *And when was it that we saw you sick or in prison and visited you?'* [40] *And the king will answer them, 'Truly I tell you, just as you did it to one of the least of these who are members of my family, you did it to me.'* [41] *Then he will say to those at his left hand, 'You that are accursed, depart from me into the eternal fire prepared for the devil and his angels;* [42] *for I was hungry and you gave me no food, I was thirsty and you gave me nothing to drink,* [43] *I was a stranger and you did not welcome me, naked and you did not give me clothing, sick and in prison and you did not visit me.'* [44] *Then they also will answer, 'Lord, when was it that we saw you hungry or thirsty or a stranger or naked or*

---

18. Metz, *Faith in History and Society*, 117.

sick or in prison, and did not take care of you?' [45] *Then he will answer them, 'Truly I tell you, just as you did not do it to one of the least of these, you did not do it to me.'* [46] *And these will go away into eternal punishment, but the righteous into eternal life."*

No Longer Keeping Up Appearances

John S. McClure

I want to begin this morning's sermon with a spiritual and theological claim: "Jesus walks among us in the actual bodies of refugees and immigrants." In verse 35 of Matthew's apocalyptic drama of the last judgment, the Son of Man, better translated the "Human One," says these words: "I was a stranger and you welcomed me," and then in verse 40, "just as you did it to one of the least of these who are members of my family, you did it to me."

Liberationist ethics begins with a theological claim—God's preferential option for and christological identification with the poor.

In Jewish tradition, it is possible to designate certain persons as actual representatives of oneself, often in a profound, substitutionary sense. The Jewish *shaliach* principle states that "a man's representative is as the man himself."[19]

What is unique here is that it is not a particular individual who is designated as a representative, but an entire group of persons: the vulnerable and powerless of the world, including the stranger, the children, the hungry, the thirsty, the most desperate and needy among us. These are actual, physical representatives of the glorified Christ, the Human One. The Christian Reformer Martin Luther interpreted this passage from Matthew by saying that poor, naked, hungry, prisoners, and strangers in our midst are, in fact "little Christs."

19. Hare, *Interpretation: Matthew*, 290.

Fred Craddock and Eugene Boring would have us notice something further about this moment in the great drama of salvation and judgment. And I quote:

> To the reader's surprise (ancient and modern) the criterion of judgment is not confession of faith in Christ. Nothing is said of grace, justification, or the forgiveness of sin. What counts is whether or not one has acted with loving care for needy people. Such deeds are not a matter of "extra credit" but constitute *the decisive criterion* of judgment.[20]

So let's see if we can find the Human Ones, the "little Christs," in our midst for a minute. In July of 2019, six reporters visited the Migrant Detention Center in Clint, Texas. Here are a few lines from their report that might help us to locate the actual bodies of the Human One in our midst:

Following Christine Smith's outline of liberationist preaching as "weeping, confession, and resistance" the sermon begins with our weeping, i.e. our awareness of the terrible plight of the powerless in our midst.

> Outbreaks of scabies, shingles, and chickenpox were spreading among the hundreds of children and adults who were being held in cramped cells, agents said. The stench of the children's dirty clothing was so strong it spread to the agent's own clothing—people in town would scrunch their noses when they left work. The children cried constantly.[21]

Now let's listen for a moment to words of the Human One in the actual voices of immigrants and refugees interviewed as part of a 2017 Kaiser Family Foundation study of immigrant families.

From the Human Ones living in Bethesda, Maryland we hear these words: "Many of us came as children, and we had no idea about the future. Now we have no option but to stay because . . . we are afraid to go back to a place that we are not familiar with."

20. Boring and Craddock, *The People's New Testament Commentary*, 94.

21. Romero, Kanno-Youngs, Fernandez, Dickerson, Borunda, and Montes, "Hungry, Scared and Sick."

From the Human One in Boston, Massachusetts we hear these words: "we wake up every morning with the fear of being deported, of the separation of our families, to have to leave the kids."

And in Chicago, the Human One speaks these words: "I am both mom and dad for my children . . . So, I must be there, and I think, God forbid it, but if I get detained, they will deport me."

And in Los Angeles: "I think everybody is a lot more scared. There's more fear in me personally speaking . . . now I feel it personally. Not before, but now I do."

Listen again to Matthew 25:40: "Just as you did it to one of the least of these . . . you did it to me." And then in verse 45 we hear the decisive words of judgment: "Truly I tell you, just as you did *not* do it to one of the least of these, you did *not* do it to me." Just as you did not welcome, did not feed, did not clothe, did not care for, did not love—you did not love the Human One. And those who did *not* do these things, we are told, "will go away into eternal punishment, but the righteous into eternal life" (v. 46).

Here we shift from weeping to confession, which is an act of conversion from one way of thinking to another.

These are not necessarily words of condemnation. They can be words of invitation and opportunity. They invite us to ask where we are in this picture— among those who do, or do not welcome; do or do not love; do or do not feed and care for. These words give us an opportunity to confess our sin and *convert* if you will—from sinful toleration of such suffering, and from sinful, arms-length acts of charity toward those who suffer such indignity, to *confessing faith in the actual historical, social, and political redemption of the suffering of the Human Ones in our midst.* This confession might run like this:

1. I confess that God is actually present in the poor immigrants in our midst—as God incarnate.

2. I confess that the God of resurrection says "No" through the church, Jesus' resurrected body, to the unjust treatment of immigrants.

3. I confess that God wants not only my charity, but my social and political advocacy for the immigrant.

4. I confess that I cannot participate *at all* in God's redemption of this world without being involved in the redemption of the suffering of the Human Ones in our midst.

Good will, good wishes, and thoughts and prayers, leave us dangling somewhere between the "you did *not* do it to me" and the "you *did* it to me" side of the equation. Actual material, social, and political commitment to saying "No" to the suffering of these Human Ones is what is ultimately required— material acts: feeding, clothing, real and tangible acts of welcoming. Such actions involve more than good will, more than

> Here, what is sought is a commitment to a historical and material project that addresses the systemic aspects of injustice.

donations, but that we work for the kinds of structural changes that will see to it that we go beyond fairness to justice in our relationship to those who have no power, no justice, no voice, no hope, no place to lay their heads.

Such faith is an act of actual *identification* with immigrants, and the confession of our own vulnerabilities, mistakes, and struggles. According to Andrés Albertsen: "Faith is not something that one gets, nor something that one has. Faith is something that one does. Faith is the ongoing work and process of identifying with the least of our brothers and sisters and of acknowledging our own vulnerabilities, mistakes and struggles."[22]

Dorothy Day, the co-founder of the Catholic Worker Movement, spoke in a *Catholic Worker* article of her own experience of a shift in perspective like this one day during her charity work, a conversion

> Dorothy Day provides a brief illustration of this kind of confession and conversion.

to a new kind of faith: "On Holy Thursday, truly a joyful day, I was sitting at the supper table at St. Joseph's House on Chrystie Street

22. Albertsen, *Sermon at Diamond Lake Lutheran Church.*

and looking around at all the fellow workers and thinking *how hope-less it was for us to try to keep up appearances.*"[23]

To decide to quit "keeping up appearances"—acting as if charity can be enough and that the situation of immigrants and poor people in our midst can be dealt with without significant, even radical, social change—this is the conversion that is required at the heart of Matthew's apocalyptic vision of the Last Judgment. This is what it means to make a decision to quit keeping up appearances. Marie Dennis says that it means that we learn "to shape our lives and futures from the standpoint and for the sake of those who are poor."[24]

Dorothy Day's writings are instructive about what is required to identify fully with the Human Ones in our midst, and to have this kind of faith. First, it requires letting go of bits and pieces of the material things that we cling to in order to secure ourselves in this world, including most of the bits and pieces of the self-induced, panic-driven security of our national borders. In 1952, Day wrote, "The main thing is not to hold onto anything."[25] Although Day surrounded herself with items of beauty, many of which were stolen, she held them lightly. She lived simply and gave up on the idea that life's greatest moment is to sit high on top of the great heap of possessions we have accumulated, or the reputation we so cherish, staring at the sunset with a cocktail in our hands. For her, the greatest joy was found in the community of love where her privileges and riches fell to the side and she experienced genuine communion with the least of these.

Here we shift from confession to resistance. It is important to illustrate what it takes to begin to live lives that are truly resistant to the current system of exploitation and oppression.

Second, this kind of faith involves challenging and changing the unjust systems that keep immigrants living in fear, keep the poor and the sojourner in our midst from the benefits of

23. Dorothy Day Guild Blog, April 18, 2014.

24. Dennis, *Diversity of Vocations*, 95.

25. Dorothy Day Guild Blog, April 18, 2014.

education, healthcare, and housing, and keep wages and labor laws inhumane. This connects, of course, with the first idea of letting go of material things, because it may mean that profit margins suffer, dividends are not as good, housing prices are not as inflated, the job market is more competitive, and taxes are a bit higher. The situation of the citizen is inextricably connected to the situation of the im-

> It is a fundamental liberationist principle that liberation of the poor is also liberation of the wealthy, and that the two are profoundly connected.

migrant, just as the situation of the wealthy is part of the same economic system that is built in many ways around cheap labor, not offering healthcare to employees, and promoting the wealth management of those who can actually afford to invest in the free market. In Matthew's apocalyptic vision, the least of these are not left out—a hand is offered to them, a real connection is made across the abyss of economic difference, there is no salvation for some without salvation for all.

And third, this kind of faith involves participation in an expansive community of commitment—one that includes the church but that cannot be defined by the limits of the church's walls. The community of faith may include social workers, politicians, public school teachers, persons from other faiths, and other advocates. This text in Matthew is often called the great text of "anonymous Christianity." The text implies that anyone who welcomes the stranger in this way,

> Unlike the witness ethic, where the church is alone as a solitary, countercultural witness community in a hostile world, the liberationist ethicist finds church wherever solidarity with the poor and powerless is expressed.

whether Christian or not, comes into a direct relationship with Jesus the Human One. According to Douglas Hare, this means that many persons who are in solidarity with the poor and the immigrant "are . . . 'in Christ' (to borrow Paul's language). . . . They are "anonymous Christians."[26] This expands tremendously our idea of when and where church meets: in a shelter, on a street

26. Hare, *Interpretation: Matthew*, 291.

corner, at a rally, in the public square, at a town hall meeting, in an immigration lawyer's office.

Recently, police officers have been turned into primary forces for deportation, resulting in record-breaking detentions and deportations. Civil rights and due process issues abound, and trust between immigrant communities and local police is increasingly strained. The most serious of the federal programs driving this is the "Secure Communities" program or S-Comm, where, if someone is flagged as undocumented, ICE sends a "detainer request" asking the local authorities to hold the person until ICE can take them into custody for deportation. S-Comm cannot work if local authorities do not honor detainer requests. As I am preaching, several coalitions of anonymous Christians, including persons of many faiths, migrant rights organizations, and community organizations, are at work persuading local law enforcement officials in high-immigration counties around the country to resist becoming ICE deputies and to be more creative in the ways they handle detainer requests. To date, they have had an enormous effect against S-Comm in Santa Clara County, California, Washington, DC, and Cook County, Illinois. This is the church in action, both confessing and anonymous, seeking real ways to welcome the Human Ones in our midst. There are many other efforts, large and small, that we can join, and there are new opportunities to live out our faith each day in service to the least of these.

> Here we show Christians and "anonymous Christians" linking arms to subvert an unjust system from within.

The living Christ, God's Human One, is incarnate in the immigrant and in all of the least of these. And God's judgment is all wrapped up with how these persons are treated. We have an opportunity today to accept the invitation in this text, to quit trying to keep up appearances.

When and Why to Use an Ethic of Liberation

An ethic of liberation is best used in situations where abuses of power and privilege are in the foreground, or in congregations in need of a better understanding of the ways power and privilege blind us to the gospel. For instance, this approach, informed by critical theories of sexual and domestic violence, would have made good sense in the wake of the Penn State child sexual abuse scandal. It might also have been effective in the immediate wake of the Charleston church shooting, or after the police killing of George Floyd, where issues of white privilege and white nationalism were present.

This approach is also needed in situations where hegemonic interpretations of biblical texts need to be challenged and reconsidered. For instance, prominent evangelical justifications of the use of violence against Muslims, based on the account of the fall of Jericho in the sixth chapter of Joshua where non-combatant adults and children are killed, might be challenged as driven by xenophobia, racism, and a willful and incorrect misreading of the text. Other such readings of texts, which are used to prop up white nationalist privilege, could be pursued within a broader hermeneutic of suspicion in order to better understand how the anti-immigration rhetoric within many American churches is oppressive or even violent. These resources go a long way in helping preachers re-interpret troubling texts, so-called "texts of terror,"[27] or texts that have been used to promote racism, economic injustice, or ableism, and provide ways to understand the influence of social location on biblical writings and contemporary interpretations.

An ethic of liberation is also well-used in situations requiring solidarity between or within communities of faith or action: interfaith community organizing gatherings, Poor People's Campaign rallies or worship services, Earth Day, International Women's Day, MLK, Jr. holiday gatherings or worship services, women's shelters, or homeless shelters. In these situations, preachers can make common cause for the liberation of an oppressed group in sermons, linking arms with many so-called anonymous Christians.

27. Trible, *Texts of Terror*.

Some congregations actively dedicate themselves to becoming more inclusive, committing to rethinking language, rituals, forms of embodiment, architecture, and mission in ways that will be welcoming to persons with disabilities, differing sexual orientations and gender identities, diverse races and ethnicities, and disparate economic backgrounds and situations. In such congregations, a liberationist ethic teaches critical theories of gender and sexuality, ability, race, ethnicity, and economics. In the process, language and practices that embody hegemonic and non-inclusive ideologies can be unearthed, critiqued, understood, and acted upon.

A liberationist ethic also works well where the preacher is concerned to bring about a theological paradigm shift toward ethical forms of theology in general within a congregation. To some extent all liberationist preaching is doctrinal preaching that seeks a conversion from spiritualized (forgiveness, justification) theologies of redemption to material/historical (liberation, justice) theologies of redemption. Such a paradigm shift can take some time to bring about, but it can have a significant impact that supports nearly every ethical approach in this book, if time is taken to preach about and toward it. This paradigm shift can also help persons of privilege crack the mirror of their own privilege and begin to see others, whose lives have been mostly peripheral, as central to the message of the gospel and to their own faith.

Situational Sermon Example: Liberation Ethic

Johanna W. H. van Wijk-Bos, Professor of Old Testament, *emerita*, was Dora Pierce Professor of Bible and faculty liaison to the Women's Center at Louisville Presbyterian Theological Seminary in Louisville, Kentucky, where she taught for more than three decades. This sermon was preached in the seminary chapel on September 15, 2006, at the height of the Iraq War. In the sermon, she asks whether we should cling any longer to patriarchal images of God and ensuing forms of faith and practice, and invites us to reimagine God in the powerful, consoling, and liberating image of Second Isaiah's woman in labor.

Isa. 42:10–17 (preacher's translation)

[10] *Sing to the Holy One a new song,*
God's praise from the ends of the earth!

You who go down to the sea and you creatures in it,
you islands and their inhabitants.
[11] *Let them cry aloud the desert and its towns,*
the settlements where nomads dwell;
let them sing who inhabit the cliffs,
from the tops of the mountains let them shout.
[12] *Let them give to God glory;*
God's praise in the islands let them declare.

[13] *The Holy God like a mighty hero goes forth,*
like a man of war stirs up his fury;
he yells even roars;
against his foes shows his power.

[14] *I have been silent for a long time,*
kept still and restrained myself;
like a woman in labor I scream,
I gasp and pant all at once.

[15] *I will scorch mountains and hills,*
cause all their greenery to wither;
I will turn rivers into islands,
and pools I will dry up.
[16] *I will cause the blind to walk*
in a way unknown.
On paths they knew not
I will make them a way.
I will turn darkness before them into light,
and rough places into level ground.
These are the things;
I will do them without fail.
[17] *They shall turn back in deepest shame—*
who trust in made images,
who say to metal castings,
"You are our gods."

Is God a Man of War?

Johanna W. H. van Wijk-Bos

Sisters and brothers in Christ: In a recent discussion with my three-and-a-half-year-old granddaughter while we were driving to her home (and we have many discussions of great importance in the car), she segued from stories about her friends, and all kinds of events both real and imagined, into a lengthy rumination that included many references to God. When I noticed that she referred to God consistently as "He," I suggested that she might want to reconsider this, as God may not be a man and can also be referred to as "She." "Oh no!" said Emma, quite indignant at the very thought. "God is a boy. He has a penis." While the vision this provided was still within my mind, she added, "He stands up," clearly referring to bathroom habits. Thus a three-year-old's logical conclusion in view of the dominant male referencing of God. We, here at the seminary and in our churches of all kinds, have of course moved far beyond the mind of the three-year-old. But it may not hurt us to contemplate once again how we name God. As Elizabeth Johnson observed in her book *She Who Is: The Mystery of God in Feminist Theological Discourse*, "The way in which a faith community shapes language about God implicitly represents what it takes to be the highest good, the profoundest truth, the most appealing beauty. Such speaking in turn powerfully molds the corporate identity of the community and directs its praxis."[28] In other words, how we think and speak about God is reflected in the way we act. It matters how we speak of God, for in speaking of God we speak of ourselves. In imagining God, we imagine ourselves.

There is no doubt that today we live in fearful times: fears of remembered events of pain and loss in our nation, fear of unknown terrors still looming on the horizon. And our leaders are well aware of the demon of fear that roams our land and will take any opportunity to renew the smoldering embers to make them blaze up anew with statements that contain lies and half-truths.

---

28. Johnson, *She Who Is*, 4.

The text we read from Isaiah 42 comes from a fearful time also. A people that trusted in God and God's presence to protect them had been ripped from their land, forcefully deported, dwindled in size. Cowering in the shadow of mighty Babylon, they can only look back at a dreaded past and forward to a fear-filled future. A scourged, abased, and insignificant group of people in the midst of the gigantic powers of the world, knows little else to do than to mourn the loss of everything they held dear.

Into the midst of this dispirited group of almost no account comes the voice of the prophet we call the Second Isaiah. Like a trumpet blast the prophet shouts words of comfort, of forgiveness, of assurance and promise. And more than any text of the Bible this singer/poet/prophet turns the focus on God. From the very first words: "Here is your God who is on the way to you," (Isa 40:9–11) to the very last invitation to a people who have nothing, people who have *absolutely* nothing, to be on their way to God (Isa 55:1–3), Second Isaiah jubilantly proclaims the rich mystery of the Holy One of Israel.

The passage we read opens with an invitation to a song:

"Sing to the holy one a new song;
God's praise from the ends of the earth!"

All humans and animals, land and sea, mountains and valleys, are to join in the praise of this God. What a notion. Just when you are busy mourning for all that is not going right, to turn your mind to the praise of God.

I'm reminded of the story that Andrew Black told in the Women's Center this week of a refugee who has AIDS. This man fled his homeland, contracted HIV during his early stay in the US, became desperately ill, and was abandoned by his family when they found out he has the virus. He has no resources, no supports that one can tell. He's not a citizen of this country and we know what that means in these days. And so, Andrew related, his mouth is filled with God's praise. He continually thanks God for God's great goodness towards him.

Turning our minds toward the praise of God in the midst of fearful events is not what might first occur to us, but it is what the text urges us to do. For, according to Second Isaiah, look at what kind of God you have. Nothing like these immobile statues they carry around in the processions in Babylon. Your God is on the move! Like a mighty hero! Like a mighty hero God goes forth! Like a Man of War, stirs up his fury! The New Revised Standard Version renders this as "warrior" but in the Hebrew it says an *ish milhamah*. It is a "man of war" we have in front of us. A passionate, powerful, warrior God who will put pain to these enemies of ours: a yelling, roaring bringer of vengeance against the foe. The cries of jubilation, of praise to God, have turned into the cries of the vengeful warrior-man.

Well, that should be a comfort to a community in sack and ashes. Here will be one who will fight for them—will fight their battles for them with god-like power and might. It's an old, familiar image on which Second Isaiah draws, one that goes back to the dawn of ancient Israel as a people when they first fled Egypt, Pharaoh and his mighty army, and on being rescued, sang together with their leader Moses: "The Holy One is a Man of War! The Holy One is his name!" "Man of War" is not a title commonly used in biblical texts, but Second Isaiah in using it draws on the significant connection with an earlier deliverance. It is comforting in fearful times to take refuge in the mighty power of God.

Oh, we may say and think it neither so crudely as my granddaughter or the Second Isaiah, but we have our own ways of praising a God of power and might, do we not? When I told Aaron, our worship assistant, the title for today's sermon, *Is God a Man of War?*, he laughed and said: "I know the answer to that!" And so we may all think that we know the answer to that: "Of course not." But although we may be uncomfortable with the phrasing, the male image of a strong God who intervenes is not alien. This is how we know God, as "king," and "Lord," and "father." It is all too human, and too understandable that we do so, for these are comforting images embedded in our tradition and our text.

But Second Isaiah is not done. Second Isaiah is not satisfied with just a reference to the past, be it ever so liberated a past. As so often this poet turns heads and minds in an entirely different direction in a shocking manner. After the roaring cries of the warrior a pent-up silence:

> "I have been silent for a long time,
> kept still and restrained myself.
> Like a woman in labor I scream,
> I gasp and pant all at once."

It is clear that we are now in entirely different company than that of the warrior-man. *Now* we hear and see very different things. From a description in the third person, the text turns to the first person: "*I* have been silent. *I* scream. *I* gasp. *I* pant." Where with the first image we heard angry battle cries, stirring up his war craze, and the foes' fear with his yelling, we now hear a silence. An expectant, held-in silence, and then we hear the screams and the panting of a woman in labor.

Both warrior and woman make a loud noise. But their screams have a very different purpose. Where the mighty hero warrior goes out to bring destruction, the woman cries out because she *brings forth life.* And in so doing, she experiences pain. Hebrew poetry frequently works with an intensification of images, and here a mighty hero becomes a man of war who in turn becomes a woman in childbirth. Both are images for God. The cries that heralded death become the cries that announce life. The one who went out against the foe is turned into one who is dependent, dependent on neighbors and community, for help with the birthing.

I am afraid that we, perhaps like ancient Israel, are all too inclined to stay with the first image, in our own way, translated into our own male naming and imagining of God, and ignore the one that the entire imagery culminates in: a vulnerable God who is in pain with the producing of life. The picture of God as a woman in labor puts God in the position of sharing in the pain of creation. It shows God as vulnerable, and as powerful at the same time as a woman about to have a baby. We note that there is no stereotyping or sentimentalizing of the female image. There is power, and risk, and energy, as well as pain for the woman in childbirth.

Of course, this is not the only female imagery of God available to us in the Bible, where God reveals Godself to Moses as "I will be who I will be." It is only one image that paints a unique picture in providing a close-up of a different kind of God than perhaps we have had in mind. If we recognize vulnerability and pain in the deity, we usually confine it to the suffering of Jesus, and if we let it touch God at all, we confine it to God's fatherhood. This text from long ago, long before Jesus, tells the people of that day, tells us, who may in Jesus lay claim to these words, "Look here! Look here people! People in pain and fear! God shares our pain. God shares our fear. Just like that of a mother in childbirth."

In closing, let me recall the observation by Elizabeth Johnson that how we speak of God powerfully molds the identity of the community and directs its actions and reflections. This was no less true of ancient Israel than it is of us. But it may for us be a matter on a different scale. We are as Christians and a nation not a small group of defeated people in the shadow of gigantic powers of the world. And it is no longer the fifth century before the Common Era. The question I believe that faces us is, "May we hang on *at all* to the image of God as that of a mighty male, as reflected in so much of our Christian naming of God, in times when our own destructive power so overshadows the future? Is a male picture of God still *at all* viable?"

Has it not proven its destructive influence in our own destructive postures toward other peoples and races, and among ourselves in numerous divisions and discriminations? Is it not time to take a different turn—a turn already taken by Second Isaiah, a turn laid out for us in the work of theologian Elizabeth Johnson, that she proclaimed from this very pulpit—a turn to a God who in our naming and imagining is seen and heard as one who stands with us in our pain, and who joins in the cries of all who suffer?

There is nothing more we can desire of God than that God stands with us in our pain. There is nothing more we can desire of each other. There is nothing more painful we can do to one another than not to stand with each other in our hurt. Hurt, and grief, and pain, are a normal part of life. It is the very mark of God's love that God knows our pain from the inside out.

May it be the very mark of our love for one another that we develop an eye for each other's woundedness, that we may hear each other's cries, and covet to carry each other's burdens rather than to strive to emulate the mighty warrior gods of our day. Perhaps it is not yet too late.

Additional Reading

Black, Kathy. *A Healing Homiletic: Preaching and Disability.*

Copeland, Jennifer E. *Feminine Registers.*

González, Justo, and Catherine González. *The Liberating Pulpit.*

Helsel, Carolyn B. *Preaching About Racism: A Guide for Faith Leaders.*

Hinnant, Olive Elaine. *God Comes Out: A Queer Homiletic.*

Kim, Eunjoo Mary. *Preaching in an Age of Globalization.*

Jackson, Cari. *For the Souls of Black Folks: Reimagining Black Preaching for Twenty-First Century Liberation.*

McClure, John S., and Nancy J. Ramsay, eds. *Telling the Truth: Preaching About Sexual and Domestic Violence.*

Smith, Christine Marie. *Preaching as Weeping, Confession, and Resistance: Radical Responses to Radical Evil.*

———. *Preaching Justice: Ethnic and Cultural Perspectives*

Travis, Sarah. "Troubled Gospel: Postcolonial Preaching for the Colonized, Colonizer, and Everyone In Between." *Homiletic* 40 no. 1 (2015) 47–55.

Turner, Mary Donovan, and Mary Lin Hudson. *Saved From Silence: Finding Women's Voice in Preaching.*

4

Hospitality Ethics

AN ETHIC OF HOSPITALITY is usually motivated by a growing aware-ness of how much more social, spiritual, and moral insight can be discovered through genuine face-to-face, collaborative conversa-tions with other human beings of all kinds. The insights that emerge in such conversations can never be fully achieved through debate, reading position papers, attending community forums, or through various social or educational media. They are only possible through actual face-to-face, body-to-body *encounter*. Only in such encoun-ters can moral understanding and solidarity be achieved and mor-ally grounded relationships flourish.

Instead of focusing on achieving moral consensus, moral virtue, or moral advocacy, the ethic of hospitality preacher wants to cultivate *relationships* grounded in moral reflection. Such rela-tionships require a model of face-to-face dialogue that welcomes different persons without attempting to override or do violence to their unique experiences of moral discernment. The Judeo-Chris-tian tradition of "hospitality to the stranger" contributes much of the biblical and theological support for this dialogical model. Key scholarly voices interpreting this tradition include Christine L. Pohl, Amos Yong, Parker Palmer, Letty Russell, Emmanuel Levi-nas, Jacques Derrida, John Caputo, and Luce Irigaray. Although these scholars diverge widely in their emphases, they all are involved, to a greater or lesser extent, in the excavation, exposition, or reinterpretation of this ethical tradition.

The tradition of hospitality to the stranger has its roots in ancient Israel. As *gērîm* (sojourners), the people of Israel experienced the host-guest relationship as a key to their own survival. After their sojourn in Egypt, during their time in the wilderness, they discovered firsthand the importance of having generous and responsive hosts. Because of this, the people of Israel reflected ethically on themselves as hosts in relation to others who needed a welcome table in order to survive or flourish: travelers, widows, orphans, and the poor. This reflection was formalized in the ethical mandate in Deuteronomy 10:19: "You shall also love the stranger, for you were strangers in the land of Egypt."

Throughout the New Testament narrative, especially as it is told in Luke's Gospel, Jesus was also at the mercy of the hospitality of others, hosted by Simon Peter, Levi, Martha, Zacchaeus, and others. Central to the New Testament tradition of hospitality to the stranger is Luke's story of The Road to Emmaus (Luke 24:13–35). This story in particular illuminates how significant it was for the host and the guest to *reverse roles* in the way that hospitality functions. In that post-resurrection story, Jesus the stranger is hosted by a weary pair of disciples. Then, in a startling moment of reversal and recognition during the breaking of bread, Jesus ceases to be guest and becomes the host (v. 31). The earliest Christian congregations, which met mostly in homes, continued this tradition. Hosts such as Philologus, Julia, Nereus, Nereus's sister Olympas, and Lydia, welcomed itinerant charismatic prophets such as Paul and Barnabas, developing partnerships with these wandering prophets in discerning together the truth regarding Jesus' life, death, and resurrection.[1]

Whereas a communicative ethic operates at the level of experience best identified as intersubjective in nature, where universal consensus is sought between strong and often well-developed subject positions, an ethic of hospitality operates at the level of the

1. See Koenig, *New Testament Hospitality*, 91–98.

interhuman. At this level of experience, vulnerable human bodies encounter one another and search less for forms of moral consensus than for forms of moral solidarity—ways of being together in the world that can decrease fear, violence, and selfish action, and promote communities of hospitality. Instead of searching for universal common ground, an ethic of hospitality strives to identify significant bits and pieces of moral truth as they emerge between persons who are, at the deepest levels, strangers to one another. The goal of this process is the creation of ethical relationships shaped by the constantly shifting rhythms of the guest-host reversal.

As Edward Farley emphasizes, the stranger is the "other," who presents us with the "mysterious presence of something which contests my projecting meanings on it, an unforeseeable depth which . . . cannot be cognitively or emotionally mastered."[2] This means that interhuman relations are always asymmetrical rather than symmetrical. The stranger knows something (many things) that I do not know and has had experiences I have not had. In some things he/she is "above" me (my host). In other matters, this relationship shifts, and I cease to be guest and become host, having certain knowledge and expertise that shifts my position in the equation. In hospitable conversations, power and leadership shift constantly back and forth based on asymmetries of knowledge, experience, or resources. This means that such conversations are never really over. The fact that participants are strangers keeps them aware of the possibility, indeed the probability, that a topic will need to be reopened. There is always more to be discovered. Moral truth is always in process and moral relationships are constantly developing.

The Way Out

For the hospitality ethicist, the fundamental problem is what Emmanuel Levinas calls "Totality"—the totalizing urge to "make

2. Farley, *Good and Evil*, 39.

same" that which is inextricably different and completely other.[3] A sinful urge resides within human beings to manipulate, control, or even obliterate that which diverges from our own way of thinking, our community of origin, or our own set of moral assumptions. This is true across all kinds of difference. The urge to make same can manifest itself in classrooms, churches, racial or ethnic enclaves, political parties, families, and in many other places and situations. Violence occurs whenever the uncontrollable mystery of another person is seized upon, controlled, stereotyped, constricted, or altered from the outside, constricting human freedom and growth. This is to forcefully take away that which makes another person human, one of God's unique created beings. This includes their unique bodily experience of the world, the way the world feels to them, their ways of knowing the world, and their ways of surviving and thriving.

According to philosopher Levinas, the aspect of a person that presents this mysterious, inviolable presence, the presence of the vulnerable stranger, is the human face *(visage)*. As a holocaust survivor, Levinas found it difficult to believe that the Nazi soldiers could look into the faces of Jewish families, and especially children, and still pronounce the word *kill*. For this reason, the commandment "Thou shalt not kill" stands at the center of Levinas's ethic of hospitality. Killing another is the ultimate act of Totality, or saming another. For Levinas, the vulnerable face says (without words), "Do not kill me."[4] The way out of saming others involves looking into human faces and living out a form of hospitality that welcomes each unique presence in the world, refusing to kill the God-given reality that each person manifests. For hospitality ethic preachers, therefore, the way out of a totalizing homiletical approach involves at least three things: meeting with others, asking others what they experience, and listening for how their responses can come to expression in the pulpit.

3. See Levinas, *Totality and Infinity*.
4. Levinas, *Totality and Infinity*, 84.

Meeting with Others

First of all, for the hospitality ethic preacher, it is crucial to enter into face-to-face, mutually welcoming encounters with those whose lives are implicated by particular ethical issues, either before, during, or after preaching. These encounters may include members of one's congregation, or the broader community, and can occur before, during, and/or after the actual event of preaching. Dialogical forms of homiletics such as "collaborative preaching"[5] or Leah Schade's "deliberative dialogue"[6] encourage small pre-sermon group Bible studies involving various persons affected by an ethical issue. Testimonial models such as Lucy Rose's homiletical "wagering"[7] or Lillian Daniel's use of individual testimonies[8] suggest inviting lay persons into the pulpit to interpret biblical texts in relation to specific ethical topics in order to hear the diverse voices within a particular community of faith. Sermon dialogue models such as Doug Pagitt's "progressional implicatory preaching"[9] or Ernesto Cardenal's *campesino* Bible discussions[10] encourage preachers to hold conversations with laity during sermons or in place of sermons. All of these methods welcome into the proclamation of the gospel the actual bodies, faces, and voices of others.

Asking Others

During these face-to-face encounters, preachers learn to *ask* persons how they are affected by an ethical issue or situation, why they are affected, what it feels like, and what they think is most important for the preacher to know about the issue from within their own realm of experience. In this sense, each human person is potentially a living oracle, someone who may bring with them

5. McClure, *The Roundtable Pulpit*.

6. Schade, *Preaching in the Purple Zone*.

7. Rose, *Sharing the Word*.

8. Daniel, *Tell It Like It Is*.

9. Pagitt, *Preaching Re-Imagined*.

10. Cardenal, *The Gospel in Solentiname*.

a sacred word that needs to be heard from the pulpit. Models of preaching that are built around an ethic of hospitality usually involve asking people what they think, either in sermon preparation groups, during sermon delivery, or in sermon forums after sermons are preached. Preachers signify to sermon listeners that it is crucial to *ask* rather than assume in order to understand how differing persons are affected by and think about particular ethical issues or concerns.

Listening to Others

Most of all, hospitality ethic preachers build careful *listening* into sermon preparation and delivery. They cultivate skills for listening to other people's ways of thinking, experiencing, and feeling. They allow this listening to move sermons in directions that may be quite divergent from the preacher's own inclinations. Sermons adopt what David Hesselgrave calls a "rhetoric of listening,"[11] where sermon listeners are invited to follow the contours of a genuine face-to-face conversation that is coming to terms with some aspect of a difficult ethical problem. This means that sermons may arrive at moral insights that are more partial and emergent than final in nature. Such sermons, however, signal to listeners that their ideas, thoughts, and feelings are important and taken into account. In other words, they are being listened into speech and welcomed into the household of faith as people whose feelings, thoughts, and experiences matter.

Hospitality ethic preachers, however, will not limit their homiletical welcome to congregation members, but will also invite others who can diversify the conversation or who have more direct experience of some aspect of the ethical issue under discussion. For instance, a preacher who is preaching on immigration might take one or two church members and visit a local immigrant relief organization and gather persons there in pre-sermon conversation about

11. Hesselgrave, "'Gold from Egypt,'" 95.

the biblical text to be preached. Or the preacher might invite such persons to offer their testimonies directly from the pulpit.

No matter how it is accomplished, the way out of totalizing interpretations of moral issues will involve actual face-to-face encounters that include a range of persons whose lives are implicated. This approach requires preachers to welcome others into the actual practice of preaching, work on their asking and listening skills, and learn how to turn preaching into a place where the rhetoric of listening is central.

The Way In

No matter what sermon model is used—whether collaborative preaching, deliberative dialogue, progressional implicatory preaching, testimony, or actual Bible discussion—several conversational features are crucial to providing a hospitable way into an ethical issue. Here, I will list a few of the key dynamics that form a part of the rhetoric of listening within hospitality ethic sermons.

Following the Dynamics of Topic-Setting

Although a broad topic such as immigration might be on the table for discussion in preparation for a particular sermon, how that topic is approached could vary widely and should not be assumed by the preacher at the outset. No matter what model of preaching is used, it is important to include several approaches to a topic as they are introduced by different persons who set or establish the topic in a distinct way. Within a collaborative sermon, such as the one in the topical example below, topic-setting dynamics that actually occurred in the pre-sermon conversation are either described or imitated in the sermon. In the *campesino* Bible discussion provided in the situational example below, we actually overhear the various participants in the Bible discussion establish perspectives on the topic at hand.

All of these dynamics provide a way into the topic that welcomes, either directly (with permission) or indirectly, participants in the pre-sermon roundtable. By extension this has the effect of welcoming sermon listeners who will recognize such topic-setting as inclusive of contrasting perspectives on the topic at hand. The way that the preacher might have wanted to set the topic is not necessarily left behind, but it is now placed within the larger context of other guests, who are also given the power to host the way in which a particular moral topic is considered. The goal is to bring authentically collaborative conversational language into the pulpit.

Providing Clarifications and Interpretations

The second way into a moral topic within an ethic of hospitality is through clarifying and interpreting the topic once it has been set. The way into the topic needs to be as clear as possible for all participants.

- What, in fact *is* immigration?
- How is an immigrant different from a refugee?

A hospitality ethic never assumes that everyone is on the same page or shares the same knowledge. Clarification is often crucial when it comes to welcoming all persons into a conversation.

Including Contrapuntals as Needed

Another dynamic occurs when a group acknowledges a particular interpretation but decides to go in another direction. David Buttrick once called this dynamic a "contrapuntal," whereby a preacher acknowledges alternative perspectives while moving in one particular direction.[12]

---

12. Buttrick, *Homiletic*, 47.

- "Although we could focus on the small percentage of immigrants who have criminal records, we are more concerned with . . ."

- "Although some of us are very concerned with protecting low-wage jobs, our group decided that . . ."

Contrapuntals remind sermon listeners that alternative directions of thought may exist, even if today's sermon has to limit its scope.

Linking and Differentiating

Conversation partners sometimes link arms and agree on a particular way of interpreting and pursuing an idea. At other times they spend time differentiating their thoughts on a topic. Individuals want to make it clear that their ideas are either the same or not the same, even though they may seem similar. Preachers can pick up on these dynamics and include them.

- "Some of us agree with . . . about . . ."

- "Our roundtable diverged widely when it came to . . ."

- "There seems to be a clear difference of thought about . . ."

Linking and differentiating dynamics remind sermon listeners that one way into an ethical issue is to work hard to locate oneself in the conversation. Ethical reflection involves a learning process that includes many back-and-forth rhythms that situate participants in different places. Linking and differentiating can also make it clear that while the community of faith is not all of one mind, it is still able to link arms occasionally on things that matter.

Repairing Ideas as Needed

Sometimes new information prompts someone to change or alter their perspective, repairing it in some way. This may involve self-disclosure, acknowledging a self-correction. Such moments, when taken up into the sermon (with permission), can help listeners also reflect on ways in which their own thinking might be repaired, or has been changed in the past.

- "I used to think . . . But after hearing what Carla said, I now believe . . ."
- "We experienced a real change of heart about . . . But it was based largely on Bob's story. Let me try to retell that."

The goal of the language of repair is to remind the community that learning takes place within the constantly shifting asymmetries of the guest-host reversal, and it is entirely possible and *permissible* to alter one's thinking. The way into a topic sometimes involves revising one's current position.

Showing How Ideas are Assessed

Assessment occurs when conversation partners begin to decide upon the value of a particular way of thinking about a difficult ethical topic. This provides a way into the topic that is valuational in nature.

- "Our roundtable group agreed that this was beginning to make better sense!"
- "I like that!"
- "Now that's a really valuable insight."

When we hear this kind of language in pre-sermon groups and in sermons, we prick up our ears and see if perhaps some genuine coming to terms is occurring that might signal some form of relational solidarity among us. It says that the way into the topic requires a willingness to assess what is of value, and an openness to claiming these assessments as possible within a larger group of people.

Empowering the Voices of Participants

The final way into a difficult topic within an ethic of hospitality is through empowering people in conversation to discover and assert their own interpretive power based on their own experiences and knowledge. Several typical dynamics of empowerment in conversations are very useful when taken up into the language of sermons.

Retelling Their Stories

Storytelling can be an important way to get a toehold in a conversation by asserting one's power vis-à-vis one's personal experiences. When hosting conversations on ethical issues, it is crucial to ask for stories from those with many perspectives on a topic. If the topic is immigration, for instance, the sermon's rhetoric of listening can include stories told by actual immigrants, ICE agents, detention officers, public health officials, and so on—inasmuch as such persons can actually be recruited into pre-sermon roundtables or dialogue sermons. When these stories are used in sermons (with permission if told in pre-sermon roundtables) they can be profoundly empowering. They invite sermon listeners who share similar experiences to also feel empowered and included.

Including Frame Resistance and Reframing

A second form of empowerment occurs when conversation partners either resist the way that a topic or idea is being framed, or work to reframe the topic in some way. An immigrant, for instance, may resist the frame "illegal," for a variety of reasons, and may prefer to reframe their situation as being "without papers," or "undocumented." It is important in hospitable sermons to hear the ways that certain frames are resisted and might be reframed. This communicates that the way into a difficult ethical topic is not set in stone, and that under-informed or poorly formulated approaches can be questioned and set aside.

Allowing Needed Interruptions

A final, more dramatic form of empowerment within difficult conversations is interruption. Interruptions are either intentional or unintentional moments of disregard for normal turn-taking transitions in conversations in order for the speaker to get in on the discussion without having to wait. This usually occurs at junctures where conversations are experienced as hurtful or completely uninformed. Such interruptions can also find their way into sermons as moments where it is crucial to stop a particular direction of thought and set the record straight.

- "I think it is important to stop here and change directions."
- "Stop! This is not right! We have to think about this differently."
- "Wait a minute. In our group Javier reminded us of . . ."

Such moments can be very welcoming for those who find themselves experiencing over and over again certain forms of uninformed stereotyping, bullying, or blatant disregard of facts. To include such interruptions communicates that our usual ways into an ethical issue can be jettisoned or reframed at any time. Participants are not always required to tiptoe around and try to locate *the* perfect moment to dispute a completely misinformed idea.

The Way Through

In face-to-face conversations, hospitality ethic preachers look for key signposts that can be preached as ways through an ethical conundrum. As noted above, these signposts are not necessarily indicators of broad universal consensus (important for a communicative ethicist) but may be better identified as ways people are able to *come to terms* with one another in relation to a specific issue. Although this might indeed include coming to terms around rational ways through a moral conflict or problem (consensus), it can also include affective, visional, relational, or volitional responses as well. In hospitable conversations, coming to terms might be identified whenever participants begin to articulate a vision, decide what needs doing, indicate priorities, make commitments, inspire one another, or decide on certain forms of action or ways to *be with and for* one another and continue to seek a way through, in spite of differences. Coming to terms takes several typical forms in hospitable conversations. These are easy to adjust and use in sermons.

Identifying Commitments

The first sign that a way through is being expressed occurs when participants in a conversation begin to identify shared commitments. A commitment is more a statement of solidarity than a statement of consensus or agreement. It communicates a willingness to act in a particular way or to continue thinking or feeling in a certain direction. For instance, someone might not rationally agree with the proposition that "every immigrant should be given all rights granted to citizens," but they might be able to commit to thinking about what rights are essential for the survival and best path forward for immigrants. Or they might commit to empathizing more with those who have no citizen rights at all.

Sharing Proposals

When a group begins to articulate proposals for thinking, feeling, or action, this can be another sign that a way through may be coming into view. Proposals often contain qualifiers such as "perhaps," "maybe," "could," "might," "I wonder," etc.

- "One thing we could do is . . ."
- "Maybe we should . . ."
- "I wonder what would happen if we . . ."

Proposals invite people to put themselves momentarily into a particular frame of mind and see how it feels, or what new insights or problems arise. They are tentative and provocative in nature and have a heuristic function, provoking discovery and further reflection on possibilities and outcomes. Proposals are always signs of a possible way through an ethical situation.

Narrating Scenarios

Scenarios project imaginative futures or test cases for suggested or emerging ethical ideas or commitments. Scenarios often have an if/then quality.

- "If we decide to admit every immigrant, then one thing that might happen is . . ."
- "If we go that way, here's one possible scenario."

Sometimes scenarios sketch out an eschatological future that might be a goal for reflection.

- "I'm imagining a world where there are no borders . . ."
- "Here's where the Bible seems to want us to be. How can we get there?"

When scenarios are being used, a way through the issue is often emerging, not as a full-blown proposition, but as a possible direction or way of seeing into the future.

Looking for Inspiration

Inspirational language often occurs when energy and enthusiasm are on the rise around a particular way of thinking, feeling, or acting.

- "This might be an energizing option for us!"
- "Many of us really seem to be able to get behind that way of thinking!"
- "I love that!"
- "We seem to really believe that!"

Inspirational language is feeling language, and it is often more attached to ways of being and acting than to ideas. Inspiration is not always positive or aspirational in nature. Sometimes we are inspired by someone's action in a difficult situation, struggle, or plight.

- "As we heard about the children in detention being cared for by teenage strangers because their parents were not there, our hearts broke! Something has to be done!"

Such language is often a signal that a way through is gaining traction or emerging.

Including Expressions of Solidarity

A final important signal of a way through occurs when a group begins to express their commitment to the people whose lives are most affected by an ethical issue, *and* to one another as concerned and increasingly involved partners with those affected persons. Levinas makes it clear that coming to terms with one another is ultimately a relational rather than an ideational reality. To discover oneself entering into an actual face-to-face relation of responsibility and/or love for an immigrant who is living in fear and without hope, no matter where one's current thoughts and beliefs currently stand, is to begin to enter into the domain of interhuman ethics itself.

- "We all seemed to be clear about one thing. We care! We want new and better lives for our immigrant friends."
- "It's complicated. But we now have 'skin in this immigrant game.' We see the human side. We want more for our immigrant friends and for ourselves."

In Levinas's understanding of the Jewish idea of hospitality ethics, "being-with" is more originary (deeper, prior) than "being." The discovery of our relationship of responsibility to the other/stranger is itself to become fundamentally ethical. There can be no ethics at a distance—only face to face. It is crucial, therefore, to look for signs of *particularized solidarity* (responsibility, care, love, concern, hope, involvement, guidance, etc.) as these begin to replace non-relation or distance. All such expressions of increasing solidarity are crucial for preaching. They signal a way through a moral issue where everyone is welcomed into a web of relationships that are diverse and ethically responsive at their core.

The Way Toward

A homiletical ethic of hospitality is oriented toward a future that is always emergent from within the organic and aesthetic rhythms of interhuman dialogue. As theologian Marjorie Suchocki puts it, God's Word is available in the world all of the time at a barely "whispered" level.[13] This whispered Word is the creative Logos, and the hospitality ethic preacher listens for this Word deep within the relational nexus of conversations centered on interpreting the biblical witness. The preacher then draws that emerging, creative, and ever-creating Logos up from the level of a whisper to the level where it can be articulated as a message of love, mercy, and hope. Preachers are essentially listening into being a Word that is *present* in our midst, while also being *ahead of where we are*, inviting us into new forms of ethical reflection and creativity that could not be otherwise anticipated. Here, preachers are not looking for utopian universals (communicative ethic), either/or ways to be fools for Christ (witness ethic), or shared social projects to initiate or join (liberationist ethic.) They are looking for here-and-now creative possibilities for moral relationships that are emerging in genuine face-to-face situations where actual ethical life-lived-together (human solidarity) is at stake.

13. Suchocki, *The Whispered Word*.

Topical Sermon Example: Ethic of Hospitality

Luke 10:27

*27 You shall love the Lord your God with all your heart, and
all your soul, and with all your strength, and with all your
mind; and your neighbor as yourself.*

Sermon Roundtable Participants:

Javier: A trained and certified plumber, Javier came to the United
States at the age of seven years old. He had Green Card immigration
status but didn't realize that it lapsed in 2010 because immigration
officials accidentally sent the notice to the incorrect address. ICE
agents showed up at his house as he was strapping his four-year-old
son into his car seat to go the church daycare. He was handcuffed
in front of his (US resident) wife and son and taken into custody.
He was detained for sixteen months at a center an eight-hour drive
away from his family, and finally won his deportation case and was
released. Now a renewed Green Card holder, he is thousands of
dollars in debt from legal fees and lost income. He volunteers at
Citizens for Immigration Reform and Support (CIRS), a regional
social service agency for immigrants.

Pamela: A social worker at a CIRS, Pamela is seminary educated and does a great deal to harness the church-based resources
in the region in support of the work of the agency. She does annual
educational events at local churches, hosts fund-raising events on
the CIRS campus, and maintains a blog devoted to providing biblical and theological perspectives on immigrant and refugee issues.

Jim: A carpenter and handyman, Jim is a long-time church
member. He has struggled in recent years to find employment at
a living wage and blames some of his situation on undocumented
immigrants who work for lower wages than he expects. He is very
generous and employs undocumented immigrants himself from
time to time, especially when a job is too large or difficult for him
to handle on his own.

John: He is a professor of preaching and a sermon writer.

The Way of Love

John McClure

Our roundtable group, whose names are in the bulletin this morning, were asked to discuss the topic of immigration in light of this text from Luke. As we started looking at this text, we wondered together whether the priority of "loving God with all your heart, all your soul, all your strength, and all your mind" could also hold some

Notice that the topic-setting for the sermon is something "we" do.

clues about the more difficult issue of "loving neighbor as ourselves." After all, as Jim pointed out, "Loving God isn't always all that easy!" When we lose a loved one to an unexpected accident or illness, or lose a job we've relied on for years, God seems distant, unapproachable, and perhaps even indifferent. When Javier was surprised by ICE agents while putting his four-year-old into his car seat to head to

Jim and Javier are empowered here, as their ideas and stories are made central to establishing this idea that loving God is sometimes difficult.

church daycare, and then sat in detention for nearly a year and a half, eight hours away from home, he remembers wondering where God was in all of that. Loving a God who would permit that to happen was tough at times.

But as Pamela reminded us, this might require us to get to know God in another way—to see God as suffering, too—suffering with the Israelites when they were slaves in Egypt, and suffering when Jesus walked the road to the Cross. God is not a puppeteer, but a fellow-traveler who leads us, nudges us, cajoles us in a

Pamela's theological re-framing provides another way of seeing God, and how God acts in the world.

particular direction—in the direction of *love*. And this is the clue we found in Luke's "love God" command: that "love God" essentially translates "love Love." Or as we translated it: "love the *Way of Love that is God*, in all things. The goal is to love that way with every aspect of our being: heart, mind, body, and soul. So the challenge when it comes to the issue of immigration seems to be learning to love neighbors in a way that moves us in the direction of the kind of Love that God has, a love that suffers with each other and will not let each other go.

Here again, the group dynamics are important: commitment, then hesitation, due to some real-life concerns. The difficulty of real-world ethical commitment moves into the foreground at this point.

We started to get really excited about this in our group, and were ready to make a strong commitment to something like this, when it began to occur to us that in lots of ways we are not really ready to commit to this kind of love. Especially if it involves loving our neighbor as ourselves. This means that the same thing we want for ourselves (love, joy, hope, security, family, peace, and our daily bread) we want for our neighbors.

Again, Javier's story (used with permission) is crucial, empowering him, and the narratives of persons similar to him, to be at the table.

Javier wondered how he could get past his anger at the immigration officials who sent his Green Card renewal papers to the wrong address, the ICE agents who chose to arrest him in front of his son and wife, the prison guards who bullied and threatened him, or the owners of the private prison company that profited from detaining him by charging exorbitant prices for food, hygiene products, and phone cards to call his family. What does it mean to move in the *Way of Love that is God* when everyone around you is moving in the way of suspicion, pride, and hate? As Jim put it, "It's a dog-eat-dog world!" Everyone is in it for themselves. Competition is stiff, and social media want to make us think that *everything* is competitive. Everything is a "zero sum game." That's the reality of things. If an immigrant on

Jim is also empowered here, as his concerns about employment and wages is given voice. The goal at this point is to welcome key voices in the interhuman conversation about immigration into the room, and into the sermon.

a Green Card from Mexico can underbid a carpenter like Jim, they get the job! What's to love about that?!

Pamela wondered if we couldn't reframe what the problem is, for both Javier and Jim. She said it was right there in their language, which points to systems and not simply to individuals: the immigration system, homeland security and ICE, the prison system, and the capitalist system in which unions are no longer viable and pricing and competition are unchecked.

> Pamela again attempts to reframe the conversation, but there isn't any uptake this time around. It is important, however, to hear her perspective about social systems and structures, so it is included.

But this idea only goes so far, as our group sees it. Because "people can still choose to avoid the Way of Love and not do what's right." And maybe it's possible with the system we currently have to act with love. No one is forcing the ICE agents to grandstand in front of Javier's children, and no one is forcing the prison guards to act like bullies. And people can choose to price their goods and services in a way that is fair for all. There's

> Here we begin to see some coming to terms occurring. Both Jim and Javier can see eye to eye when it comes to individual moral responsibility.

still an individual factor in there somewhere, as Jim put it. The Way of Love can still be followed in situations and systems that are not always ideal.

In fact, there was some energy and enthusiasm in our group over a really amazing idea—*that we might let the Way of Love help us rethink the systems we currently have to make them better.* So, if you're an immigration official, you could create a system to doublecheck to see if you have the correct address, because you don't want to traumatize an immigrant family. Or if

> Here the accent falls on the *affective* element: shared enthusiasm that is also beginning to take the shape of a proposal for action.

you're an ICE agent, you might create a humane arrest or registration policy that is not humiliating. If you're a prison guard, you institute best practices for avoiding and reducing bullying. And if you're a prison company managing a detention facility, you ensure that there are purchasing options that do not price gouge. And if you're a carpenter you create a social network that welcomes Mexican immigrants with carpentry skills. It might even be possible to expand this social network to other carpenters in the area and use it as a way to discuss fair pricing and quality control in one's community in order to improve the standard of living for all.

Not all of us will be completely happy with this approach, and would prefer to get rid of the current systems altogether. But it does seem to suggest important areas where our social systems can be improved or changed entirely. There doesn't seem to be any conclusive reason that these systems *have* to be cutthroat, cruel, antagonistic, and hateful. Children don't *have* to be separated from their parents at the border. Another way is possible. We don't *have* to label undocumented immigrants as "illegals." Identifying and registering undocumented workers at chicken processing plants doesn't *have* to be conducted as a military raid with zip ties used as handcuffs. Treating others as ourselves could be possible, even with our current system. Or at least it seemed to us, as we wrestled together with this issue.

What do you think? This idea is only a modest proposal. And maybe our scenarios are overly optimistic. This love commandment may require a more nuanced approach. Or a revolution. We just wanted to start the conversation. Let's see where it goes from here.

Various scenarios are put on display, as the group (and those hearing the sermon) paint pictures of possible changes of practice that might occur.

Here, some frame resistance is identified, which both Pamela and I had voiced in the roundtable.

But, ultimately, in the roundtable, and here in the sermon, the focus on individual responsibility is embraced—at least as a good starting point.

Finally, the conversation is opened up. There might be a forum time during the service or afterward, or sermon listeners can simply reflect further on their own with this brief conversation starter in mind.

When and Why to Use a Hospitality Ethic

An ethic of hospitality is best used in situations where more ethically responsible and generative *relationships* are needed. As an interhuman ethic, an ethic of hospitality focuses primarily on creating and enhancing relationships that can sustain and improve ethical reflection and action. By getting people face to face and inviting them to engage in actual conversations about ethical issues that have a significant impact on their lives, preachers hope not only to discover new pathways forward, but to achieve new or enhanced forms of relational solidarity. This approach, therefore, might work in contexts of immediate, consistent, and unavoidable moral distress such as detention-center towns near the Mexican border, mining communities in West Virginia, or urban neighborhoods undergoing rapid gentrification. Leah Schade, for instance, discovered that sermons grounded in "deliberative dialogue" were generative of significant creative ethical commitment in a community struggling to make theological and ethical sense of fracking.[14] In her experience it was crucial to have pre-sermon face-to-face engagement by those on all sides of the issue, in order to identify new forms of commitment to one another that would also reflect a commitment to protecting and preserving God's creation. Only through such encounters could commitments be discovered and maintained.

An ethic of hospitality is also a good way for preachers to signal that they respect and value the perspectives, feelings, and ideas of others in the moral leadership of congregations and local communities. The approach signals to lay persons that their ideas, insights, and experiences are of significant value in both the interpretation of the gospel and in guiding the community's life together. This approach, therefore, shifts some of the authority for moral leadership into the hands of those whose lives will be most affected by moral decisions.

At the same time, this approach teaches lay persons that they can be ethical and theological interpreters of biblical texts

---

14. Schade, *Preaching in the Purple Zone.*

and life. As they hear their interpretations, feelings, commitments, aspirations, and ideas proclaimed from the pulpit, it is hoped that they begin to take more responsibility and assume more authority as biblical interpreters and lay theologians. It is a good approach to use, therefore, in situations where preachers desire to empower lay persons to think reflectively about difficult ethical issues in light of the biblical witness.

An ethic of hospitality is also important in situations where it is clear that important voices are *not* being heard in the public moral debates that are currently underway. Vulnerable *human experiences* of a moral issue may have not yet become clearly articulated *subject positions* on the issue. Many people all around us are struggling to achieve subjectivity. Their unique moral experience hasn't yet been articulated as a clear, rational, and debatable public position. This means that certain people feel unwelcomed and, in fact, completely left out of many larger moral conversations. Because it works at the interhuman, rather than intersubjective, level, an ethic of hospitality is able to unearth these emerging subject positions and give them a meaningful voice. Those whose experiences are unique and complex are welcomed as important contributors within difficult moral conversations.

Finally, an ethic of hospitality is well used in situations where persons of differing ethical viewpoints rarely gather face to face. Experiential and ideological siloing has increased in the age of social media, and an ethic of hospitality can sometimes be a good way to counteract some of the effects of this situation. By getting persons whose experiences and viewpoints differ together in conversations where they are valued as both guests and hosts, and where they can actually hear their own voices proclaimed as important for discerning the gospel, an ethic of hospitality confronts and challenges the assumptions behind much of our current ideologically driven virtual reality. It makes human vulnerability more present and real and adds significant complexity to the way that moral conversations have to be both framed and understood. In the end, it reinvigorates the relational and affective aspect of moral deliberation that often goes missing in the current online environment.

Situational Sermon Example: Hospitality Ethic

The Gospel in Solentiname is the transcription of discussions of biblical texts in a fishing community on an island of the Solentiname Archipelago in Lake Nicaragua during the mid-1970s, when the dictator oligarch Anastasio Somoza DeBayle was in power. The community was founded by Ernesto Cardenal, who was both a priest and a poet. In 1967 Cardenal organized discussion groups focused on biblical texts, inviting group members to discuss these texts in light of their life situation. Phillip Berryman, who had the opportunity to participate in the group, noticed that "gradually the process of dialogue was broadened and more explicitly social and political dimensions were brought in. . . . Having begun as an attempt in some ways to repudiate Somocista society and to escape from it, the Solentiname community became a focal point of resistance to it."[15] *The Gospel in Solentiname* is composed primarily of group discussions recorded between 1971 and 1976, transcribed and edited by Cardenal. Berryman observes that "usually the setting is the chapel on Solentiname, but occasionally it is another island. The presence of the lake, whether calm or stormy, is usually felt. Often enough the Mass takes place after a meal of beans and rice, or fish from the lake, or perhaps roast pig. Someone reads the Gospel selection as a whole and then it is commented on by verses or sections."[16]

Mark 4: 21–25

[21] He said to them, "Is a lamp brought in to be put under the bushel basket, or under the bed, and not on the lampstand? [22] For there is nothing hidden, except to be disclosed; nor is anything secret, except to come to light. [23] Let anyone

15. Berryman, *The Religious Roots of Rebellion*, 9. Most of my description of Cardenal's life and of the Solentiname community in the foregoing passages are culled from Berryman's excellent descriptive overview at 7–10.

16. Berryman, *The Religious Roots of Rebellion*, 9.

with ears to hear listen!" [24] *And he said to them, "Pay at-tention to what you hear; the measure you give will be the measure you get, and still more will be given you.* [25] *For to those who have, more will be given; and from those who have nothing, even what they have will be taken away."*

The Lamp

Ernesto Cardenal

Sermon/Dialogue 46

This gospel we heard at a Mass on Mancarroncito, the last and most remote island of the Solentiname Archipelago. The Mass was at the home of Doña Yoya, under an arbor. Facing us, a blue cove. Far away, in the middle of the lake, the small, solitary island of Zanata, and farther away, as if emerging from the water, the two volcanoes of the large island of Ometepe. We came to say Mass at Mancarroncito because it is far removed from the rest of the archipelago, and those who live there, very poor and with very few boats, can seldom get to our little church.

> *He also said to them: Does anyone bring a lamp to put it under a bushel or under a bed? No, the lamp is put up high, where it will give light.*

I explained that "bushel" was a basket to measure grain, like what Nicaraguan farmers call a *medio* or a *cuartillo*.

FELIX said: "I think the gospel is a very high doctrine that God has offered to humanity to give us all light. That's why it's like a raised lamp."

Someone from Mancarroncito: "Jesus never went around hiding. That's the light on high. And we have to be like that, too. Not hide with the truth but bring it out into the light."

JULIO MAIRENA: "People who have hidden justice are the ones who hide the light. Christ came for the poor. But often the priests, because they're getting the money of the rich, have hidden this message for the poor. And that's the light under the bushel, under the grain basket. There are others who, through fear of the powerful, apply the gospel only to their private lives, and that's the light under the bed, it seems to me. The one who raises the light high is the one who protests against injustice."

FELIPE: "Not only the priests. We also hide the light. We also have the duty to preach the truth, and many times we don't speak it out of fear. And we have to speak the truth, even though they threaten us, or attack us, or kill us, as has always happened with the prophets."

ALEJANDRO: "We have come now to have this meeting on Mancarroncito Island and to comment here on the gospel. And I see this as bringing out the lamp so it will shine. People from here will also mobilize for other places, for somewhere else, carrying that light that we always have to bring out from under the bushel. Bring it out so that it will shine for everyone."

REBECA: "The lamp is Christ. Because he said: "I am the light." Anyone who reads the Gospel and then hides the book in a drawer is hiding the light. Anyone who reads it and then tells about it to someone else is bringing out the light so it can be communicated to another neighbor. And that's the way Christ's word is communicated, like a light from which you light other light."

FILEPE: "We make that light shine with friendship, making one island friendly with another. Putting an end to the separation and the isolation that there is on our islands. This light will give good light when we feel ourselves all united like a single island. We transmit the light to each other with friendship, with union. We communicate Christ when we communicate friendship. The light, then, is love."

OLIVIA: "Yes, when we're isolated we don't communicate the message of the Gospel, which is a message of unity, of brotherhood. We brothers and sisters have to form a community of love. They followed Christ. He preached and there were crowds who followed him and there was a lot of love there among them. And we are gathered together here illuminated by that Gospel."

Well, nothing of what is hidden will remain uncovered;
and there is no secret that will not be revealed. You who
have ears, listen.

JULIO: "It seems to me that this has now been fulfilled. The priest used to read the gospel in Latin, and they said things nobody could understand. But now many of us are clear about what the gospel means and about what we're looking for: What we're looking for is to be equal."

I said: "In reality this was the great secret that had to be made public at some time. The Gospel was revolutionary, but what was revolutionary and subversive in it was kept hidden for a long time."

OSCAR: "Christianity means sincerity, to be clean, to love without hypocrisy. Being revolutionary is putting an end to lying. That's why Christ came, so nothing would be hidden. So there would be light. Now society lives with falseness and lies, like somebody that has their lamp underneath the bed."

Pay attention to what you hear. The same measure that
you use to measure, God will use it to measure you also;
and he will give even more to you who hear. For to him
who has will be given more; but from him who has not will
be taken even the little that he has.

FELIX: "Can that be fair? I don't understand why that's so. I want it explained."

Old TOMAS PEÑA: "It seems to me that those who have, who are the rich, God gives them more so they'll increase their capital, which for them is their life and their glory. And he gives it to them to ruin them. And he is going to take from the poor even the little they have so as to give them true glory. Because the poor are the ones who are going to follow him. That's what he's trying to make clear, it seems to me."

FELIPE, his son: "I think just a little different. People who are stuck on money have no belief in God even though they think they do. God's going to take away from these guys what little belief they have in him, the tiny bit of love of God. The ones that have, and that receive even more, are the ones that love. These God is surely going to fill more with love."

Several people said they liked what Felipe had said, that it was true. OLIVIA commented: "That's the way I understand it. It seems to me that the ones who have the most love, more love will be given to them. And the ones who have little love, all love will be taken away from them. They will be separated from humanity so they don't get in its way."

And one of the young people from Mancarroncito: "As I understand it, the ones who don't have any love here on earth have nothing even though they think they do. But anyone who has love is rich, and they'll be given more. I think that's the way it is, right?"

An old man from this island: "Those who are generous, with every service they do to others they get richer in their generosity. They become more generous. And those who have nothing of that get poorer and poorer. Those who are cruel, with each cruelty they get crueler and crueler."

FELIX MAYORGA: "The rich have a saying: Money creates money. And it's true that the richer you are, the more money you make. And what about us? The poorer the *campesinos* are, the poorer their harvests are. We not only don't earn, we lose. So the rich get richer and richer, and the poor get poorer. That must seem like an injustice but that's the way it is. And the kingdom of heaven is also like that, as I see it."

JULIO: "He has said that, with the same *cuartillo* or the same *medio* that we measure with, we're going to be measured, and that we'll be given even more. He means that the love that we give we receive, and we receive even more. And also the hatred or the cruelty that we give, we receive that, and we receive even more."

OLIVIA: "He also says that people who have ears should hear. The ones who listen are the ones who already have some love in their hearts, and they're given more love. The ones who don't listen (because they have nothing) will lose what little they had. That's why the ones who have the most love will increase their love, and the selfish ones will become more miserable."

I said that we had clearly seen that just as money creates more money love creates more love and selfishness creates more selfishness. I also said that this light that today's Gospel speaks of is the light we have brought to Mancarroncito, and it's the same one that has illuminated us in this reading. With this light things have emerged that were hidden, what was hidden in the Gospel has been revealed to us.

OSCAR: "That is clear. It's coming out, we're all seeing what was hidden."

The noonday sun blazed in the sky. The lake was an intense blue. Some distance away, a little sail boat. And in the background, the distant volcanoes of the Island of Ometepe.

Additional Reading

Allen, Ronald J., John S. McClure, and O. Wesley Allen, eds. *Under the Oak Tree: The Church as a Community of Conversation in a Conflicted and Pluralistic World.*

Daniel, Lillian. *Tell It Like It Is: Reclaiming the Practice of Testimony.*

McClure, John S. *The Roundtable Pulpit: Where Leadership and Preaching Meet.*

Moiso, Aimee. "Standing in the Breach: Conflict Transformation and the Practice of Preaching." *Homiletic* 45 no. 1 (2020) 13–22.

Palmer, Parker. *The Company of Strangers: Christians and the Renewal of America's Public Life.*

Rose, Lucy Atkinson. *Sharing the Word: Preaching in the Roundtable Church.*

Russell, Letty. *Church in The Round: Feminist Interpretation of the Church.*

———. *Just Hospitality: God's Welcome in a World of Difference.*

Schade, Leah. *Preaching in the Purple Zone: Ministry in the Red-Blue Divide.*

Conclusion

As we have seen, each ethical approach in this book operates at a different level of moral experience. A communicative ethic functions at the intersubjective level, a witness ethic at the level of human virtue, a liberation ethic at the social level, and a hospitality ethic at the interhuman level. At this juncture, it is helpful once again to pause from reading and ask the following questions: (1) Do I want to engage experience at the level where Christians are addressing arguments between well-developed positions regarding a moral issue? If so, then I need an intersubjective approach such as a communicative ethic. (2) Do I want to engage experience at the level where a unique form of moral agency must be taught and practiced in order to confront demonic forces in the world today? If so, then a virtue or character development approach such as a witness ethic is clearly best. (3) Do I want to engage experience at the level where social systems and hegemonic forces must be challenged and resisted? If so, then a social approach such as a liberation ethic is called for. (4) Do I want to engage experience at the level where relationships grounded in shared ethical discernment are desired? If so, then an interhuman or relational approach such as a hospitality ethic is best.

I hope that by now it is clear that these are each distinct levels of homiletical engagement that are appropriate in different contexts and situations. Preachers will be well-served by making an informed decision about what they are trying to accomplish and how to go about that task. Once we have decided on the best approach to use, there is a rich body of literature available to assist us.

But making this decision may not be enough. Many of us need some form of ongoing reflection, accountability, and feedback to ensure that our preaching remains on the right path. I am a firm believer in peer coaching as a good way to achieve this. In my experience, there is no better way to hone our skills as preachers in and for the particular contexts we actually inhabit. Peer groups not only share the same reading and resources with me, they also commit to *learn my situation*. Because of this, they can help me dig into the details of my situation and into the intricacies of my efforts to engage a particular level of moral experience there. They can also challenge me to consider other approaches if and when my situation changes. I strongly recommend involvement in a peer group of some kind, that is committed to providing ongoing feedback and reflection.

The promise of this kind of ethical discernment and ongoing reflection is *focus*. We are no longer adrift and simply trying things out to see what works. We decide what our situation requires, what level of moral experience we are addressing, and what approach is best. We then read deeply into that approach and seek ongoing feedback to ensure that we are doing what we set out to do in the best ways possible. The result is clarity and focus—we know what we are doing and why.

No matter what process we ultimately adopt in order to hone our ethical practice of preaching, I hope that this handbook is helpful as a way of sorting out the options and understanding how they work. Preaching always engages lived experience and the ways we act in the world. As we have seen, lived experience is complex, and forms of action multifaceted. We practice preaching in the midst of a troubled world in need of careful and focused engagement with God's Word. We can do that. And we can do it well.

It's a matter of choosing an approach: a way out of sin and trouble, a way into ethical engagement, a way through difficult ethical terrain as bearers of good news, and a way toward new ways of thinking, relating, and acting in the world.

Bibliography

Abumrad, Jad. *Dolly Parton's America, Episode 6*: "The Only One for Me, Jolene," 32:21. https://podcasts.apple.com/us/podcast/dolly-partons-amer ica/id1481398762.

Albertsen, Andrés. *Sermon at Diamond Lake Lutheran Church—3/12/17—2nd Sunday in Lent*. https://drive.google.com/file/d/0B8SJC6ItnhwwRklQR3 Q2bXZLX3M/view.

Allen, Ronald J., John S. McClure, and O. Wesley Allen, eds. *Under the Oak Tree: The Church as a Community of Conversation in a Conflicted and Pluralistic World*. Eugene, OR: Cascade, 2013.

Azarian, Bobby. "An Analysis of Trump Supporters has Identified 5 Traits." *Psychology Today Blog*. https://www.psychologytoday.com/us/blog/mind-in-the-machine/201712/analysis-trump-supporters-has-identified-5-key-traits.

Berryman, Phillip. *The Religious Roots of Rebellion: Christians in Central American Revolutions*. Maryknoll, NY: Orbis, 1984.

Bishop, Bill. *The Big Sort: Why the Clustering of Like-Minded America is Tearing Us Apart*. Boston: Mariner, 2009.

Black, Kathy. *A Healing Homiletic: Preaching and Disability*. Nashville: Abingdon, 1996.

Blitzer, Jonathan. "A Veteran ICE Agent, Disillusioned with the Trump Era, Speaks Out." *The New Yorker*, July 24, 2017. https://www.newyorker.com/news/news-desk/a-veteran-ice-agent-disillusioned-with-the-trump-era-speaks-out.

Boring, M. Eugene, and Fred B. Craddock. *The People's New Testament Commentary*. Louisville: Westminster John Knox, 2010.

Brown, Sally. *Sunday's Sermon for Monday's World: Preaching to Shape Daring Witness.* Grand Rapids: Eerdmans, 2020.

Brueggemann, Walter. *Cadences of Home: Preaching Among Exiles.* Louisville: Westminster John Knox, 1997.

———. *Interpretation: A Bible Commentary for Teaching and Preaching, Genesis.* Atlanta: John Knox, 1982.

Burghardt, Walter J. *Preaching the Just Word.* New Haven, CT: Yale University Press, 1998.

Buttrick, David G. *Homiletic: Moves and Structures.* Philadelphia: Fortress, 1987.

Campbell, Charles L. *Preaching Jesus: New Directions for Homiletics in Hans Frei's Postliberal Theology.* Grand Rapids: Eerdmans, 1997.

———. *The Word Before the Powers: An Ethic of Preaching.* Louisville: Westminster John Knox, 2002.

Campbell, Charles L., and Johann H. Cilliers. *Preaching Fools: The Gospel as a Rhetoric of Folly.* Waco, TX: Baylor University Press, 2012.

Cardenal, Ernesto. *The Gospel in Solentiname.* Maryknoll, NY: Orbis, 2010.

Clary, Sheela. "Smug, Mean, and Contemptuous is No Way to Go Through 2020, Friends." *The Berkshire Edge,* January 2, 2020. https://theberkshireedge.com/smug-mean-and-contemptuous-is-no-way-to-go-through-2020-friends/.

Coffin, William Sloane. *The Collected Sermons of William Sloane Coffin: The Riverside Years, Vols. 1 and 2.* Louisville: Westminster John Knox, 2008.

Cone, James. *A Black Theology of Liberation.* 2d ed. Maryknoll, NY: Orbis, 1986.

Copeland, Jennifer E. *Feminine Registers: The Importance of Women's Voices for Christian Preaching.* Eugene, OR: Cascade, 2014.

Daniel, Lillian. *Tell It Like It Is: Reclaiming the Practice of Testimony.* New York: Rowman and Littlefield, 2005.

Davis, Dawn Rae. "Unmirroring Pedagogies: Teaching with Intersectional and Transnational Methods in the Women and Gender Studies Classroom." *Feminist Formations* 22 no. 1 (Spring, 2010) 136–62.

Dawn, Marva. *Reaching Out Without Dumbing Down: A Theology of Worship for this Urgent Time.* Grand Rapids: Eerdmans, 1995.

Day, Dorothy. *The Dorothy Day Guild Blog,* April 18, 2014. http://dorothydayguild.org/her-words-holy-thursday/.

De la Torre, Miguel A. *The Politics of Jesús: A Hispanic Political Theology.* Lanham, MD: Rowman and Littlefield, 2015.

Dennis, Marie. *Diversity of Vocations.* Maryknoll, NY: Orbis, 2008.

Eisen-Martin, Tongo. "Tongo Eisen-Martin's Brief but Spectacular Take on Poetry as Revolution." *PBS NewsHour,* February 13, 2020. https://www.youtube.com/watch?reload=9&v=zMWORqLt8FQ.

Farley, Edward. *Good and Evil: Interpreting a Human Condition.* Minneapolis: Augsburg Fortress, 1990.

Flavell, John. *The Development of Role-Taking and Communication Skills in Children.* New York: John Wiley and Sons, 1968.

Florence, Anna Carter. *Preaching as Testimony*. Louisville: Westminster John Knox, 2007.

Forbes, James. *Whose Gospel? A Concise Guide to Progressive Protestantism*. New York: New, 2010.

Frei, Hans. *The Eclipse of Biblical Narrative: A Study in Eighteenth and Nineteenth Century Hermeneutics*. New Haven, CT: Yale University Press, 1980.

Gilbert, Kenyatta R. *Exodus Preaching: Crafting Sermons about Justice and Hope*. Nashville: Abingdon, 2018.

González, Justo, and Catherine González. *The Liberating Pulpit*. Eugene, OR: Wipf and Stock, 2003.

Gramsci, Antonio. *Selections from the Prison Notebooks*. Translated by Quentin Hoare and Geoffrey Nowell Smith. Newark, NJ: International, 1971.

Habermas, Jürgen. "Morality and Ethical Life: Does Hegel's Critique of Kant Apply to Discourse Ethics?" In *Kant and Political Philosophy: The Contemporary Legacy*, edited by Ronald Beiner and William James Booth, 320–36. New Haven, CT: Yale University Press, 1993.

———. *On the Pragmatics of Social Interaction*. Translated by Barbara Fultner. Cambridge, MA: MIT Press, 2001.

Hare, Douglas. *Interpretation: A Bible Commentary for Teaching and Preaching, Matthew*. Louisville: Westminster John Knox, 1993.

Helsel, Carolyn B. *Preaching About Racism: A Guide for Faith Leaders*. St. Louis: Chalice, 2018.

Hesselgrave, David. "'Gold from Egypt': The Contribution of Rhetoric to Cross-Cultural Communication." *Missiology: An International Review* 4 (1976) 89–102.

Hinnant, Olive Elaine. *God Comes Out: A Queer Homiletic*. Cleveland: Pilgrim, 2007.

Hochschild, Arlie Russell. "I Spent Five Years with Some of Trump's Biggest Fans. Here's What They Won't Tell You." *Mother Jones*, September/October 2016. https://www.motherjones.com/politics/2016/08/trump-white-blue-collar-supporters/.

Jackson, Cari. *For the Souls of Black Folks: Reimagining Black Preaching for Twenty-First Century Liberation*. Eugene, OR: Pickwick, 2013.

Johnson, Elizabeth. *She Who Is: The Mystery of God in Feminist Theological Discourse*. New York: Crossroad, 2002.

Kim, Eunjoo Mary. *Preaching in an Age of Globalization*. Louisville: Westminster John Knox, 2010.

Kim, Grace Ji-Sun, and Susan M. Shaw. *Intersectional Theology: An Introductory Guide*. Minneapolis: Fortress, 2018.

King, Martin Luther, Jr. *A Gift of Love: Sermon from "Strength to Love" and other Preachings*. Foreword by Coretta Scott King. Boston: Beacon, 2012.

Koenig, John. *New Testament Hospitality: Partnership with Strangers as Promise and Mission*. Eugene, OR: Wipf and Stock, 2001.

Levinas, Emmanuel. *Totality and Infinity: An Essay on Exteriority*. Translated by Alphonso Lingis. Pittsburgh: Duquesne University Press, 1969.

Lindbeck, George. *The Nature of Doctrine: Religion and Theology in a Postliberal Age*. Louisville: Westminster John Knox, 1984.

Lloyd, Vincent. "Thick or Thin? Liberal Protestant Public Theology." *Journal of Religious Ethics* 42 (2014) 335–56.

MacIntyre, Alasdair. *After Virtue: A Study in Moral Theory*. 3rd ed. Notre Dame, IN: University of Notre Dame Press, 2007.

McClure, John S. "In Pursuit of Good Theological Judgment: Newman and the Preacher as Theologian." In *Loving God With Our Minds: The Pastor as Theologian*, edited by Michael Welker and Cynthia Jarvis, 202–19. Grand Rapids: Eerdmans, 2004.

———. *The Roundtable Pulpit: Where Leadership and Preaching Meet*. Nashville: Abingdon, 1995.

———. *Speaking Together and With God: Liturgy and Communicative Ethics*. Minneapolis: Fortress Academic, 2018.

McClure, John S., and Nancy J. Ramsay, eds. *Telling the Truth: Preaching About Sexual and Domestic Violence*. Cleveland: United Church, 1998.

McCray, Donyelle. "Quilting the Sermon: Homiletical Insights from Harriet Powers." *Religions* 9 (2) 1–7.

Mead, George Herbert. *Mind, Self, and Society: From the Standpoint of a Social Behaviorist*. Chicago: University of Chicago Press, 1967.

Metz, Johann Baptist. *Faith in History and Society*. Translated by D. Smith. London: Burns & Oates, 1980.

Miller, Richard Brian. *Terror, Religion, and Liberal Thought*. New York: Columbia University Press, 2010.

Moiso, Aimee. "Standing in the Breach: Conflict Transformation and the Practice of Preaching." *Homiletic* 45 no. 1 (2020) 13–22.

Mountford, Roxanne. *The Gendered Pulpit: Preaching in American Protestant Spaces*. Carbondale, IL: Southern Illinois University Press, 2005.

Mumford, Debra. *Envisioning the Reign of God: Preaching for Tomorrow*. Valley Forge, PA: Judson, 2019.

Otto, Rudolph. *The Idea of the Holy*. Translated by John W. Harvey. New York: Oxford University Press, 1958.

Pagitt, Doug. *Preaching Re-Imagined: The Role of the Sermon in Communities of Faith*. Grand Rapids: Zondervan, 2005.

Palmer, Parker. *The Company of Strangers: Christians and the Renewal of America's Public Life*. New York: Herder and Herder, 1983.

Papadopoulos, Dimitris, and Vassilis S. Tsianos. "After Citizenship: Autonomy of Migration, Organizational Ontology and Mobile Commons." In *Protesting Citizenship: Migrant Activisms*, edited by Imogen Tyler, 178–96. New York: Routledge, 2017.

Rauschenbusch, Walter. *Theology for the Social Gospel*. New York: Abingdon, 1917.

Resner, André, Jr. *Just Preaching: Prophetic Voices for Economic Justice*. St. Louis: Chalice, 2003.

Romero, Simon, Zolan Kanno-Youngs, Manny Fernandez, Caitlin Dickerson, Daniel Borunda, and Aaron Montes. "Hungry, Scared and Sick: Inside the Migrant Detention Center in Clint, Tex." *New York Times*, July 9, 2019. https://www.nytimes.com/interactive/2019/07/06/us/migrants-border-patrol-clint.html

Rose, Lucy Atkinson. *Sharing the Word: Preaching in the Roundtable Church.* Louisville: Westminster John Knox, 1997.

Russell, Letty. *Church in The Round: Feminist Interpretation of the Church.* Louisville: Westminster John Knox, 1993.

———. *Just Hospitality: God's Welcome in a World of Difference.* Louisville: Westminster John Knox, 2009.

Samuels, Eddie. "No Place for Hate Summit Teaches Tolerance." *The Atlanta Jewish Times*, January 22, 2020. https://atlantajewishtimes.timesofisrael.com/no-place-for-hate-summit-teaches-tolerance/.

Saunders, Stanley P., and Charles L. Campbell. *The Word on the Street: Performing the Scriptures in the Urban Context.* Grand Rapids: Eerdmans, 2000.

Schade, Leah. *Preaching in the Purple Zone: Ministry in the Red-Blue Divide.* New York: Rowman and Littlefield, 2019.

Schleiermacher, Friedrich. *The Christian Faith.* 3rd ed. London: Bloomsbury T&T Clark, 2016.

Slessarev-Jamir, Helene. *Prophetic Activism: Progressive Religious Justice Movements in Contemporary America.* New York: New York University Press, 2011.

Smith, Christine Marie. *Preaching as Weeping, Confession, and Resistance: Radical Responses to Radical Evil.* Louisville: Westminster John Knox, 1992.

———. *Preaching Justice: Ethnic and Cultural Perspectives.* Eugene, OR: Wipf and Stock, 2008.

Snarr, C. Melissa. *All You That Labor: Religion and Ethics in the Living Wage Movement.* New York: New York University Press, 2011.

Stringfellow, William. *An Ethic for Christians and Other Aliens in a Strange Land.* 3rd ed. Waco, TX: Word, 1979.

Suchocki, Marjorie. *The Whispered Word.* St. Louis: Chalice, 1999.

The Theology and Worship Ministry Unit, Presbyterian Church USA and the Cumberland Presbyterian Church. *Book of Common Worship.* Louisville: Westminster John Knox Press, 1993.

Thomas, Frank. *How to Preach a Dangerous Sermon.* Nashville: Abingdon, 2018.

———. *Surviving a Dangerous Sermon.* Nashville: Abingdon, 2020.

Thompson, Lisa L. *Ingenuity: Preaching as an Outsider.* Nashville: Abingdon, 2018.

Tillich, Paul. *Dynamics of Faith.* New York: Perennial Classics, 2001.

Travis, Sarah. *Metamorphosis: Preaching After Christendom.* Eugene, OR: Cascade, 2019.

————. "Troubled Gospel: Postcolonial Preaching for the Colonized, Colonizer, and Everyone In Between," *Homiletic* 40 no. 1 (2015) 47–55.

Trible, Phyllis. *Texts of Terror: Literary-Feminist Readings of Biblical Narratives*. Minneapolis: Fortress, 1984.

Turner, Mary Donovan and Mary Lin Hudson. *Saved From Silence: Finding Women's Voice in Preaching*. St. Louis: Chalice, 1999.

Webber, Robert. *Liturgical Evangelism*. New York: Morehouse, 1992.

Weil, Simone. *Gravity and Grace*. New York: Routledge Classics, 2002.

Wogaman, J. Philip. *Speaking the Truth in Love: Prophetic Preaching to a Broken World*. Louisville: Westminster John Knox, 1998.

Willimon, William H. *The Intrusive Word: Preaching to the Unbaptized*. Grand Rapids: Eerdmans, 1994.

————. Untitled sermon preached at the Ocean City Tabernacle, April 7, 2010. Accessed on Vimeo, https://vimeo.com/13362055.

Willimon, William H., and Stanley Hauerwas. *Preaching to Strangers: Evangelism in Today's World*. Louisville: Westminster John Knox, 1992.

Wink, Walter. *Engaging the Powers: Discernment and Resistance in a World of Domination*. Minneapolis: Fortress, 1992.

Made in the USA
Monee, IL
10 April 2021

65265213R00090